Formalism and Marxism

Russian Formalism and Marxist criticism had a seismic impact on twentieth-century literary theory and the shockwaves are still felt today. First published in 1979, Tony Bennett's *Formalism and Marxism* created its own reverberations by offering a ground-breaking new interpretation of the Formalists' achievements and demanding a new way forward in Marxist criticism.

The author first introduces and reviews the work of the Russian Formalists, a group of theorists who made an extraordinarily vital contribution to literary criticism in the decade following the October Revolution of 1917. Placing the work of key figures in context and addressing such issues as aesthetics, linguistics and the category of literature, literary form and function and literary evolution, Bennett argues that the Formalists' concerns provided the basis for a radically historical approach to the study of literature. Bennett then turns to the situation of Marxist criticism and sketches the risks it has run in becoming overly entangled with the concerns of traditional aesthetics. He forcefully argues that through a serious and sympathetic reassessment of the Formalists and their historical approach, Marxist critics might find their way back on to the terrain of politics, where they and their work belong.

Addressing such crucial questions as 'What is litera⁺   ' should it be studied and to what end?', *Formalism an⁴ ⁱ   as which should be considered by any stud~   ʋides a particular challenge to those   ʰ a new afterword, this classic text ,   int for those new to the field, as v   ,on in twentieth-century literary thec

Tony Bennett is Professor of ,   ᴜ ᴜpen University, UK. He is the author of *Culture: A Reforn.   ᴜᴄience* (1998) and *Outside Literature* (1990).

IN THE SAME SERIES

Alternative Shakespeares 1, Ed. John Drakakis
Alternative Shakespeares 2, Ed. Terence Hawkes
Post-Colonial Shakespeares, Ed. Ania Loomba and Martin Orkin
Re-reading English, Ed. Peter Widdowson
Rewriting English, Janet Batsleer, Tony Davies, R. O'Rouke and Chris Weedon
English and Englishness, B. Doyle
Linguistics and the Novel, Roger Fowler
Language and Style, E. L. Epstein
The Semiotics of Theatre and Drama, Keir Elam
Structuralism and Semiotics, Terence Hawkes
Superstructuralism, Richard Harland
Deconstruction ed. 2, Christopher Norris
Formalism and Marxism, Tony Bennett
Critical Practice, Catherine Belsey
Dialogism, Michael Holquist
Dialogue and Difference: English for the Nineties, Ed. Peter Brooker/Peter Humm
Literature, Politics and Theory, Ed. F. Barker, P. Hulme, M. Iversen and D. Loxley
Popular Fictions: Essays in Literature and History, Ed. Peter Humm, Paul Stigant and
   Peter Widdowson
Criticism and Society, Ed. Imre Salusinszky
Fantasy, Rosemary Jackson
Science Fiction: Its Criticism and Teaching, Patrick Parrinder
Sexual Fiction, Maurice Charney
Narrative Fiction: Contemporary Poetics, Shlomith Rimmon-Kenan
Metafiction: The Theory and Practice of Self-Conscious Fiction, Patricia Waugh
Telling Stories: A Theoretical Analysis of Narrative Fiction, Steven Cohan and Linda Shires
Poetry as Discourse, Anthony Easthope
The Politics of Postmodernism, Linda Hutcheon
Subculture, ed. 2, Dick Hebdige
Reading Television, John Fiske and John Hartley
Orality and Literacy, Walter J. Ong
Adult Comics, An Introduction, Roger Sabin
The Unusable Past, Russell J. Reising
The Empire Writes Back, Bill Ashcroft, Gareth Griffiths and Helen Tiffin
Translation Studies ed. 2, Susan Bassnett
Studying British Cultures, Susan Bassnett
Literature and Propaganda, A. P. Foulkes
Reception Theory, Robert C. Holub
Psychoanalytic Criticism, Elizabeth Wright
The Return of the Reader, Elizabeth Freund
Sexual/Textual Politics, Toril Moi
Making a Difference, Ed. Gayle Greene and Coppélia Kahn

AVAILABLE AS A COMPLETE SET (in Hardback only): ISBN 0415–29116–X

Tony
Bennett

Formalism and Marxism

Routledge
Taylor & Francis Group

LONDON AND NEW YORK

To my father and mother, with thanks

First published 1979 by Methuen & Co. Ltd
Reprinted three times

Reprinted in 1989
by Routledge
11 New Fetter Lane, London EC4P 4EE
29 West 35th Street, New York NY 10001

This edition first published 2003
by Routledge
11 New Fetter Lane, London EC4P 4EE

Simultaneously published in the USA and Canada
by Routledge
29 West 35th Street, New York NY 10001

Routledge is an imprint of the Taylor & Francis Group

© 1979, 2003 Tony Bennett

Typeset in Joanna by RefineCatch Ltd, Bungay, Suffolk
Printed and bound in Great Britain by
TJ International Ltd, Padstow, Cornwall

British Library Cataloguing in Publication Data
A catalogue record for this book is available from the British Library

Library of Congress Cataloging in Publication Data
A catalog record for this book has been requested

ISBN 0–415–32150–6 (hbk)
ISBN 0–415–32151–4 (pbk)

Contents

GENERAL EDITOR'S PREFACE   vii
ACKNOWLEDGEMENTS   ix

PART ONE Formalism revisited   1

1   Criticism and literature   3
    Questions of language   3
    Questions of literature   5
    Questions of aesthetics   8

2   Formalism and Marxism   15
    Russian Formalism: theoretical perspectives   15
    Reassessing Formalism   21
    Historical perspectives on Russian Formalism   24
    New directions in Marxist criticism   30

3   Russian Formalism: clearing the ground   36
    Linguistics and literature   36
    The question of literariness: criticism and its object 38
    The system and its elements: form and function   41
    Against the 'metaphysic of the text'   46
    The problem of literary evolution   50

4 Formalism and beyond 53
  The accomplishments of Formalism 53
  Saussure's magic carpet 57
  Bakhtin's historical poetics 61
  'Literature' as a historical category 67

PART TWO Marxist criticism: from aesthetics to politics 75

5 Marxism versus aesthetics 77
  Formalism: a lost heritage 77
  Marxist criticism: aesthetics, politics and history 80
  Literature's 'non-said' 86

6 Science, literature and ideology 90
  On practices 90
  On ideology 91
  On science 96
  On art and literature 97

7 The legacy of aesthetics 103
  The lessons of Formalism 103
  A new idealism 106
  Criticism and politics 111

8 Work in progress 116
  The post-Althusserians 116
  Modes of literary production 121
  Literature and the social process 127

9 Conclusion 137

AFTERWORD 143
NOTES 157
BIBLIOGRAPHY 168
INDEX 175

GENERAL EDITOR'S PREFACE

No doubt a third General Editor's Preface to *New Accents* seems hard to justify. What is there left to say? Twenty-five years ago, the series began with a very clear purpose. Its major concern was the newly perplexed world of academic literary studies, where hectic monsters called 'Theory', 'Linguistics' and 'Politics' ranged. In particular, it aimed itself at those undergraduates or beginning postgraduate students who were either learning to come to terms with the new developments or were being sternly warned against them.

New Accents deliberately took sides. Thus the first Preface spoke darkly, in 1977, of 'a time of rapid and radical social change', of the 'erosion of the assumptions and presuppositions' central to the study of literature. 'Modes and categories inherited from the past' it announced, 'no longer seem to fit the reality experienced by a new generation'. The aim of each volume would be to 'encourage rather than resist the process of change' by combining nuts-and-bolts exposition of new ideas with clear and detailed explanation of related conceptual developments. If mystification (or downright demonisation) was the enemy, lucidity (with a nod to the compromises inevitably at stake there) became a friend. If a 'distinctive discourse of the future' beckoned, we wanted at least to be able to understand it.

With the apocalypse duly noted, the second Preface proceeded

viii GENERAL EDITOR'S PREFACE

piously to fret over the nature of whatever rough beast might stagger portentously from the rubble. 'How can we recognise or deal with the new?', it complained, reporting nevertheless the dismaying advance of 'a host of barely respectable activities for which we have no reassuring names' and promising a programme of wary surveillance at 'the boundaries of the precedented and at the limit of the thinkable'. Its conclusion, 'the unthinkable, after all, is that which covertly shapes our thoughts' may rank as a truism. But in so far as it offered some sort of useable purchase on a world of crumbling certainties, it is not to be blushed for.

In the circumstances, any subsequent, and surely final, effort can only modestly look back, marvelling that the series is still here, and not unreasonably congratulating itself on having provided an initial outlet for what turned, over the years, into some of the distinctive voices and topics in literary studies. But the volumes now re-presented have more than a mere historical interest. As their authors indicate, the issues they raised are still potent, the arguments with which they engaged are still disturbing. In short, we weren't wrong. Academic study did change rapidly and radically to match, even to help to generate, wide reaching social changes. A new set of discourses was developed to negotiate those upheavals. Nor has the process ceased. In our deliquescent world, what was unthinkable inside and outside the academy all those years ago now seems regularly to come to pass.

Whether the *New Accents* volumes provided adequate warning of, maps for, guides to, or nudges in the direction of this new terrain is scarcely for me to say. Perhaps our best achievement lay in cultivating the sense that it was there. The only justification for a reluctant third attempt at a Preface is the belief that it still is.

TERENCE HAWKES

ACKNOWLEDGEMENTS

This is my first book and, in writing it, I have learned – somewhat to my surprise – just how much of a collective undertaking a book really is. Whilst I must accept final responsibility for any errors of fact or interpretation that remain, I owe a real debt of thanks to those who commented on the book during the various stages of its production and, in so doing, helped me to remove at least some of its weaknesses.

I am particularly indebted to Professor Terence Hawkes of University College, Cardiff – first, for giving me the opportunity to write this book and, second, for the detailed and painstaking criticisms he made of my early drafts. If I have succeeded at all in communicating my thoughts in a relatively direct and easily accessible way, this is due in no small part to the extraordinarily active contribution which Professor Hawkes has made as the editor of the *New Accents* series.

Next, I should like to thank those friends and colleagues at the Open University who commented on earlier versions of the book: in particular, Janet Woollacott and Grahame Thompson. To my brother Michael I owe thanks for both his encouraging comments and for, as ever, spotting where I was skating on thin ice. I should also like to record my debt to Professor Graham Martin of the Open University: my book would be the poorer but for the benefit I have derived from discussing with him some of the questions raised within it.

Thanks are also due to Pauline O'Mara and Sheila Beevers for their help in typing the final version of the book. And I would like to make special mention of Mike Richardson of the Open University: without his help and support, this book might never have seen the light of day.

Finally, and above all, my thanks to Sue for all her help and understanding and to Tanya, Oliver and James for providing the distractions.

Since writing the above, I have received further comments on my book from Terry Eagleton of Wadham College, Oxford, and Stuart Hall of Birmingham University. I am grateful to both of them for the helpful and friendly spirit in which they offered their criticisms.

Part One

Formalism revisited

1

CRITICISM AND LITERATURE

QUESTIONS OF LANGUAGE

This study addresses itself to three related tasks. First, it sets out to introduce the work of the Russian Formalists, a group of literary theorists who made an extraordinarily vital and influential contribution to literary criticism during the decade or so after the October Revolution of 1917. Second, by arguing for a new interpretation of their work, it suggests that the Formalists should be viewed more seriously and sympathetically by Marxist critics than has hitherto been the case. Finally, as an undercurrent running beneath these concerns, it argues that many of the difficulties in which Marxist criticism currently finds itself can be traced to the fact that it has never clearly disentangled its concerns from those of traditional aesthetics. We hope, in part, to remedy this by proposing, on the basis of a critical re-examination of the work of the Formalists, a new set of concerns for Marxist criticism, a new concept of 'literature', which will shift it from the terrain of aesthetics to that of politics where it belongs.

Wide-ranging though these concerns are, they all revolve around the same set of questions: What is literature? By what methods should it be studied? Or, more radically: Is the category of 'literature' worth sustaining? If so, for what purposes? Much of our time will be taken up in reviewing some of the different ways in which these questions have been answered and in examining their implications for the ways in which literary criticism should be conceived and conducted.

We must therefore be clear about what is involved in questions of this nature. For they are not questions which might be resolved empirically by generalizing from the similarities which those texts customarily regarded as 'works of literature' seem to have in common. They are, rather, questions about language or, more specifically, about the specialized theoretical languages or discourses of literary criticism and the functioning of the key terms, especially the term 'literature', within such discourses. Some understanding of language and of its implications for the nature of the discourses of literary criticism is therefore called for if we are both to put and respond to such questions in the appropriate terms.

This is only apparently a digression. For linguistics, once a somewhat recondite area of inquiry, now occupies a central position within the social and cultural sciences. At the level of method, techniques of analysis deriving from Ferdinand de Saussure's pioneering work on language have substantially influenced all areas of inquiry where the role of language and culture is seen to be central.[1] Similarly, at a philosophical level, the widening influence of linguistics has produced a heightened awareness of the role played by language in the process of inquiry itself. Especially important here is the light linguistics has cast on the relationship between the specialized theoretical languages or discourses of the various sciences and the 'objects' of which they speak.

For the moment, it is the latter of these influences which concerns us. Baldly summarized, Saussure's central perception was that language *signifies* reality by bestowing a particular, linguistically structured form of conceptual organization upon it. What the signifiers of language – the sound structures of speech and the notations by which these are represented in writing – signify, Saussure argued, are not real things or real relationships but the concepts of things, the concepts of relationships, each signifier deriving its meaning from its relationship to other signifiers within the system of relationships mapped out by language itself. The 'objects' of which language speaks are not 'real objects', external to language, but 'conceptual objects' located entirely within language. The word 'ox', according to Saussure's famous example, signifies not a real ox but the concept of an ox, and it is able to do so by virtue of the relationships of similarity and difference which define its position in relation to the other signifiers comprising modern English. There is no intrinsic connection between the real ox and the word 'ox' by virtue of which the meaning of the latter is produced. The relationship between the signifier and signified is arbitrary: that is, it is a matter of convention.

This is not to deny that there exists a real world external to the signifying mantle which language casts upon it. But it is to maintain that our knowledge or appropriation of that world is always mediated through and influenced by the organizing structure which language inevitably places between it and ourselves. Oxen exist. No one is denying that. But the concept of an 'ox' as a particular type of domesticated quadruped belonging to the bovine species – a concept through which, in our culture, we appropriate the 'real ox' – exists solely as part of a system of meaning that is produced and defined by the functioning of the word 'ox' within language.

The difficulty is that, although bestowing a signification, a particular conceptual organization on reality, language constantly generates the illusion that it reflects reality instead of signifying it. The organization of the relationships between objects in the world outside language appears to be the same as the organization of the relationships between the concepts of objects within language and, indeed, the latter appears to be the mere mirroring of the former.

QUESTIONS OF LITERATURE

What has been said about language in general applies just as much to the specialist languages or discourses of literary criticism. These, too, are significations of reality and not reflections of it: particular orderings of concepts within and by means of language which entirely determine the ways in which written texts are accessible to thought.

Thus, if we put the question: 'What is literature?' this can only mean: what concept does the term 'literature' signify? What function does it fulfil and what distinctions does it operate within language? Everything depends on the context within which the term is used. At the most general level, it simply denotes 'that which is written' and refers to all forms of writing, from *belles lettres* to graffiti. In a second and more restrictive usage, it refers to the concept of fictional, imaginative or creative writing, including both 'serious' and 'popular' genres, as distinct from, say, philosophical or scientific texts.

According to its most distinctive usage within literary criticism, however, 'literature' denotes the concept of a special and privileged set of fictional, imaginative or creative forms of writing which, it is argued, exhibit certain specific properties that require special methods of analysis if they are to be properly understood. It is this concept of 'literature' that we find reflected in the concerns of aesthetics. I shall henceforward represent this concept as 'literature' throughout the remainder of this chapter. If literary criticism has to do with the eluci-dation and explanation of those specifically 'literary' qualities which are felt to distinguish a selected set of written texts within the field of imaginative writing in general, then clearly such a practice requires a legitimating 'set of rules', an aesthetic, which will propose criteria for distinguishing between the 'literary' and the 'non-literary' in this special sense.

When we speak of 'literature' in this way, we are not speaking of some objective and fixed body of written texts to which the word 'literature' is applied merely as a descriptive label. We are rather speak-ing of a concept – the concept of a circumscribed set of texts felt to be of special value – which exists and has meaning solely within the discourses of literary criticism. This is not to say that the actual texts to which this concept is applied – the commonly received 'great tradition', say – exist only within such discourses. What is in dispute is not the material existence of such texts but the contention that, in any part of their objective and material presence, they declare themselves to be 'literature'. Written texts do not organize themselves into the 'literary' and the 'non-literary'. They are so organized only by the operations of criticism upon them. Far from reflecting a somehow natural or spontaneous system of relationships between written texts, literary criticism organizes those texts into a system of relationships which is the product of its own discourse and of the distinctions between the 'literary' and the 'non-literary' which it operates.

As we shall see, this contention is fully substantiated by the history of the term 'literature' which finally achieved the range of meaning discussed above only during the nineteenth century, side by side with the consolidation of literary criticism and aesthetics as autonomous and academically entrenched areas of inquiry. Meanwhile, it is important to note that the particular meaning attributed to the word 'literature' may vary to the extent that schools of literary criticism frequently differ with regard to their conceptions as to precisely what the distinguishing features of 'literature' are and, accordingly, the methods required to elucidate them. Thus it may be argued, as in idealist aesthetics, that a particular type of sensibility uniquely distinguishes the genuinely 'literary' text and that the discernment of this sensibility is achieved through empathy or intuition. Or it may be argued, as did the Russian Formalists, that the uniqueness of 'literature' consists in its tendency to 'defamiliarize' experience and that the true concern of literary scholarship should be to analyse the formal devices by means of which such an effect is achieved. Finally, this time in the camp of Marxism, it may be argued, as Louis Althusser, Pierre Macherey and Terry Eagleton have done, that 'literature' is uniquely defined by its capacity to reveal or rupture from within the terms of seeing proposed by the categories of dominant ideologies. The concern of Marxist criticism, according to this definition of 'literature', thus becomes that of understanding the formal processes through which literary texts work upon and transform dominant ideological forms.

Different criticisms, then, propose different concepts of 'literature', although all agree that 'literature' is to be defined as, in one sense or another, a special type of writing which needs to be dealt with by a special level of theorizing. In so doing, they also produce their own concerns in relation to such 'literary' works: their own constructions of the essential tasks of criticism and of the means by which these should be pursued. Ultimately, the 'literature' with which different critical traditions deal is not the same 'literature'. Even where there is broad agreement about precisely which texts are to be regarded as 'literary', these may be held to be 'literary' in quite different ways and may, accordingly, be approached and studied from quite different perspectives with often radically different aims in view.

It is tempting, faced with such competing definitions of 'literature' and of the critical task, to ask: 'Which is correct?' But, if what has been said so far holds true, there can be no way of answering this question. For there is no such 'thing' as *literature*, no body of written texts which self-evidently bear on their surface some immediately perceivable and indisputable literary essence which can be invoked as the arbiter of the relative merits of competing traditions of literary criticism.

In place of asking which is correct, then, we need to examine how these different concepts of 'literature' function within the critical discourses of which they form a part and to assess them in terms of the lines of inquiry they open up. There is, however, from a Marxist perspective, a more primary set of questions that need to be asked: Does Marxism need a concept of 'literature' at all? Does it need an aesthetic? Can it have the one without the other?

It is to a preliminary consideration of these matters that we now turn. In doing so, however, it should be borne in mind that such questions are not resolvable with reference to what literature *is* but depend on what the term 'literature' *signifies*, or might *be made to signify*, as a term within Marxist theory.

QUESTIONS OF AESTHETICS

If the line of argument pursued so far gives rise to difficulties, this is in part because it runs contrary to the empiricist assumptions of the dominant forms of English and American criticism according to which written texts are held to sort themselves spontaneously into the 'literary' and the 'non-literary'. Let me be clear, then, about what I am and am not saying. I am not maintaining that those texts which, by common agreement, are referred to as 'literature' do not exist. To the contrary, such texts have an objectively verifiable material presence *as texts*, and it is important not to lose sight of this. Nor am I maintaining that the particular types of writing associated with those texts display no special properties which would justify or make useful their designation as a distinctive set of texts within the sphere of imaginative writing in general. Indeed, this is the central point I wish to debate. What I am maintaining is that the designation of such texts as 'literature' is not a response to a property that is internal or natural to them but a signification that is bestowed on them from without by the practice of criticism.

Why is this important? Partly because, within the practical conduct of many schools of criticism, the conceptual procedures whereby they construct their object – the concept of 'literature' with which they operate – are normally hidden from view. The criticism of F. R. Leavis is a case in point. In his essay 'Literary Criticism and Philosophy', he suggests that the appropriate questions for the critic to put to any given text are:

> 'Where does this come? How does it stand in relation to . . .? How relatively important does it seem?' And the organization into which it settles as a constituent in becoming 'placed' is an organization of similarly 'placed' things, things that have found their bearings with regard to one another, and not a theoretical system or system determined by abstract considerations.[2]

Here, the labour of criticism effaces itself completely as the organization into which the critic places the text is represented as being a direct reflection of the way in which those texts are 'placed' in relation to one another *independently of his/her discourse*. Such a criticism thus 'naturalizes' both itself and its object. Its object, those selected written texts which are conceived as 'literature', is represented as a pre-given world of similarly 'placed' *things*, whereas criticism, far from being an actively constructing discourse, represents itself as a simple mirroring of the real within language.

Speaking more positively, however, such considerations naturally raise questions with regard to the validity or usefulness of the category of 'literature'. A certain degree of caution is advisable here. That the concept of 'literature' exists solely as a term within the discourses of criticism is no reason to dispense with it – all concepts only exist within specific discourses. But nor is this any reason to retain it. Rather than pre-empt the issue, we should examine how the concept has functioned within the history of criticism and assess its usefulness in terms of the types of approach to written texts which it permits and those which it prohibits. These sorts of questions are increasingly being raised by both Marxist and non-Marxist scholars, who feel that the historically relative way of viewing culture that is embodied in the concept of 'literature' is both unhelpful and outdated. Unhelpful, because from the point of view of historical studies it artificially separates the study of 'literary' texts from adjacent areas of cultural practice. Outdated, because it fails to do justice to the changing face of cultural practice induced by the reorganization of cultural production associated with the development of the mass media.

It was in this respect that we raised the question: Does Marxism need a concept of 'literature'? To avoid misunderstanding, what is at issue here is not whether Marxists should concern themselves with the study of those texts conventionally designated as 'literary', but whether they should concern themselves with those texts within the framework of a theory of 'literature' as such. Marxists have always been concerned, and rightly, to calculate the political effects of such texts and to devise methods of analysis whereby their production – alongside that of other cultural forms – might be explained as part of a materialist theory of ideology. But it is not so clear that the treatment of such texts as 'literary', as a separated system of cultural practice, or the development of an associated aesthetic is necessary or even helpful to the development of such concerns. Indeed, as most aesthetic theories seek to establish the specific nature of the aesthetic mode as a *universal* and *eternal* form of cognition, there are good reasons for supposing that such a concern would not sit too comfortably with the essentially *historical* and *materialist* theoretical orientation of Marxism.

Yet the fact is that all of the major theoretical contributions to the history of Marxist criticism contain a theory of 'literature' and a legitimating conception of the specific nature of the aesthetic mode of appropriation of reality. Lukács, for example, distinguishes aesthetic from scientific knowledge by arguing that, in contradistinction to the conceptual abstractions of science, art constitutes an anthropomorphic form of cognition which 'truthfully' depicts reality with a vivid, human-centred poetic concreteness.[3] Similarly, the 'Althusserians' – Althusser himself, Macherey and Eagleton – have broached the question of the specificity of the aesthetic mode by construing it as a form of cognition that is mid-way between the 'knowledge' of science and the 'misrecognition' of reality said to be contained in ideology. Although there are real differences between these two positions, they share the same fundamental concerns: the distinguishing of the aesthetic from the non-aesthetic, of the 'literary' from the 'non-literary'.

They both constitute 'literature' as a particular form of cognition which, if its specific nature is to be understood, requires the development of an autonomous level of theorizing within Marxism – a theory of 'literature' as a specialist sub-region within a general theory of ideology.

It is only recently that this assumption has been challenged. In their more recent work, Étienne Balibar and Pierre Macherey have argued that, in its attempts to produce an aesthetic, Marxism has responded not to its own theoretical and political needs but to the ideological demands placed on it by the need to compete with bourgeois criticism.[4] The result, they allege, is that Marxist criticism has tended to proceed by bringing Marxist categories to bear upon a set of problems that was already given to it by the bourgeois critical tradition, instead of using Marxist categories to transcend those debates by producing a new set of problems, a new approach to written texts within which the question of the specific nature of 'literature' would be no longer visible as a problem or would at least be differently formulated.

Similar reservations have been expressed by Raymond Williams. In his two most recent works – *Keywords* (1976) and *Marxism and Literature* (1977) – Professor Williams has shown how, through a protracted process of development, the word 'literature' gradually assumed its current meaning. Whereas it had earlier been used to refer to all forms of learned or scholarly writing – including philosophy and history as well as fictional forms – 'literature', as a term referring to a restricted and privileged set of fictional writing, came into accepted usage only during the nineteenth century. Prior to that there was, to put it bluntly, no 'literature' in the sense that we now tend to use that word. True, the texts of Shakespeare and Marlowe, of Richardson and Fielding existed. But they were not inserted within or perceived through the system of distinctions established by the concept of 'literature' as it has subsequently come to be defined.

Professor Williams further demonstrates how this process was connected with related transformations in such concepts as 'culture' and 'civilization' and, indeed, how the cultural vocabulary we have inherited from the nineteenth century, with its distinctions between 'high culture', 'mass culture' and 'popular culture', was related to a particular historical configuration of economic, political and ideological relationships. In short, he suggests that the organization into which certain forms of imaginative writing are compressed by the concept of 'literature' reflects a historically and ideologically produced way of viewing the texts concerned and their relationship to neighbouring areas of cultural practice.

What conclusions does Professor Williams draw from this? Let us first see how he views the problem:

> The theoretical problem is that two very powerful modes of distinction are deeply implanted in modern culture. These are the supposedly distinctive categories of 'literature' and of 'the aesthetic'. Each, of course, is historically specific: a formulation of bourgeois culture at a definite period of its development. . . . But we cannot say this merely dismissively. In each mode of distinction, and in many of the consequent particular definitions, there are elements which cannot be surrendered, either to historical reaction or to a confused projective generalization. Rather, we have to try to analyse the very complicated pressures and limits which, in their weakest forms, these definitions falsely stabilized, yet which, in their strongest forms, they sought to emphasize as new cultural practice.[5]

Williams suggests, then, that the distinctions posited by the concepts of 'literature' and 'the aesthetic' should be reviewed critically to see if, suitably reformulated, they might be of value. Proceeding in this way, he suggests that, whilst the concept of 'the aesthetic' should be discarded, the concept of 'literature' might usefully be retained if it is used to refer to a *particular, historically determined* form of writing, defined by the major literary forms of bourgeois society, instead of, as is customarily the case, to a set of universal attributes which *all* major forms of writing, from Homer to Kafka, are held to have in common.

Thus, in discussing traditional aesthetic theories, he argues that the effect of their concern with the specific nature of the aesthetic, with the policing of the conceptual boundaries between the 'literary' and the 'non-literary', is to abstract literary texts from the social and cultural processes within which they are inevitably contained, severing the connections which link them to other forms of cultural practice. With regard to the concept of 'literature', however, he writes:

Yet the crucial theoretical break is the recognition of 'literature' as a specializing social and historical category. It should be clear that this does not diminish its importance. Just because it is historical, a key concept of a major phase of a culture, it is decisive evidence of a particular form of the social development of language. Within its terms, work of outstanding and permanent importance was done, in specific social and cultural relationships.[6]

This is no mere empty dispute about words. What is being proposed here is a concept of literature that is incommensurable with the concept of 'literature' as it has traditionally functioned within the discourses of literary criticism. It refers not to the concept of a privileged set of texts which exemplify a universal and eternal aesthetic form of cognition but to a *specific practice of writing*, bound, circumscribed and conditioned by the historical, material and ideological conditions of its production. Although such texts may exhibit properties different from those displayed by other forms of writing, they are distinguished from them not aesthetically but *as one practice of writing amongst others.*

Used in this way, the term 'literature' exists no longer as a term within the discourse of aesthetics. The distinctions which it establishes are of a social and historical, not an aesthetic nature. It suggests an approach to so-called literary texts which will construe them, not as the manifestations of some abstract and universal literary essence, but as the product of a historically particular conduct of the practice of writing.

This is an important step to take. Indeed, it is a vital step for Marxist criticism if it is to approach written texts from a consistently historical and materialist standpoint. The question is: Can such a category of 'literature' be substantiated? Is it useful, from the point of view not of aesthetics but of a historical poetics, to reserve the term 'literature' for the dominant forms of bourgeois writing as a historically limited category referring to a particular type of cultural practice?

It is in an attempt to answer these questions that we now turn to consider the work of the Russian Formalists and, later, that of the Althusserians. By juxtaposing these two traditions we hope, if not to answer these questions, at least to suggest the directions in which answers might be sought.

Yet, at first glance, the route we have chosen might seem an unlikely one. For both the Formalists and the Althusserians would seem to propose precisely that form of discourse about 'literature' as abstracted and separate that Raymond Williams has been seeking to displace. The work of the Formalists has been traditionally disparaged within Marxist circles as the very apogee of aestheticism, whereas the essential concern of the Althusserians has been to distinguish between Literature, Science and Ideology as irrevocably separate categories. But it is also true that, although both traditions have been concerned to develop an autonomous theory of 'literature' as such, this attempt has, in both cases, broken down. The result, in the work of the 'Bakhtin school' in Russia in the late 1920s and, in the case of the Althusserians, in work that is still going on, has been the emergence of new traditions of inquiry which shift Marxist criticism onto an ultimately non-aesthetic terrain.

2

FORMALISM AND MARXISM

RUSSIAN FORMALISM: THEORETICAL PERSPECTIVES

Although the roots of Russian Formalism go back to the 1880s, it existed as an identifiable critical movement only during the years immediately preceding the October Revolution of 1917 and in the decade or so succeeding it.[1] Yet the term 'movement' is misleading. For the Formalists could not be described as members of a unified school of critical thought working, from an organizational basis, toward the realization of an agreed programme or manifesto. Indeed, even the name 'Formalism' was not of their choosing but was a pejorative label applied to them by their opponents in the turbulent critical arena of post-revolutionary Russia.[2]

The so-called Formalists, then, were merely a group of like-minded scholars – Viktor Shklovsky, Boris Eichenbaum, Jurij Tynyanov and Roman Jakobson were perhaps the most prominent – who shared theoretical interests in common. The only organizational bases of the 'movement' were the Moscow Linguistic Circle, founded in 1915 and headed by Jakobson, and the Society for the Study of Poetic Language (*Opoyaz*), founded in 1916 and dominated by Shklovsky. For the greater part of their histories, these bodies were largely discussion circles and, at most, bases for co-operative publishing ventures. There were, furthermore, important differences of theoretical stress and orientation between these two centres. Although both groups were substantially influenced by the developing methods of linguistics, this was more true of the Moscow Linguistic Circle than of *Opoyaz*. Similarly, whilst the concern of *Opoyaz* was fairly single-mindedly with the specific distinguishing features of European *belles lettres*, the members of the Moscow Linguistic Circle were also interested in the study of Russian folklore.

Nevertheless, the two groups did share sufficient ground for us to gloss over these differences for the moment. Two concerns stand to the fore. First, they were united in their wish to establish the study of literature on a scientific footing, to constitute it as an autonomous science using methods and procedures of its own. This entailed, as their primary concern, the question of 'literariness': that is, the problem of specifying those formal and linguistic properties which could be said to distinguish literature and poetry from other forms of discourse, and particularly from prosaic or ordinary language.

It was with respect both to the way in which this concern was pursued and the nature of the conclusions they proposed that the label of 'formalism' was applied to the Formalists. For, at the level of method, they held that the question of literature's specificity could be resolved solely with reference to the formal properties of literary texts. It was not necessary, they argued, to take into account the historical forces operative in the construction of such texts – an assumption that was to bring them into conflict with the developing schools of Marxist criticism in Russia. More substantively, in common with other schools of formalist criticism – Anglo-American New Criticism is perhaps the closest parallel[3] – the Russian Formalists tended to underwrite the Kantian doctrine of 'art for art's sake'.

This position was most fully developed in Jakobson's writings on poetry. According to Jakobson, the mode of functioning of the poetic word is such as to secure the primacy of its aesthetic over its communicative function. The question of the word's referential meaning – its relationship to whatever it signifies – which is dominant in ordinary language, is suspended in poetry where, Jakobson argues, the word is installed within an incessant play of meaning upon meaning. This process yields an excess of signification which, going beyond the mundane uses of the word, is said to be of value purely for its own sake.[4]

Second, the Formalists aimed to undermine the cogency of the concern with mimesis in literary theory by arguing that literature was not and could not be a *reflection* of reality but only a particular, semiotically organized *signification* of it. Far from reflecting reality, the Formalists argued, literary texts tend to 'make it strange', to dislocate our habitual perceptions of the real world so as to make it the object of a renewed attentiveness. Indeed, they argued that it was this ability to defamiliarize the forms through which we customarily perceive the world that uniquely distinguished literature from other forms of discourse. The vast majority of their studies accordingly set out to reveal the formal mechanisms whereby this effect of defamiliarization was produced.

Thus, at one level, they subjected particular sentences or verse structures to meticulous analysis in order to reveal the precise nature of the transformations which they effected on the categories of ordinary language. Take, as a brief example, the following sentence from Len Deighton's *Billion-Dollar Brain*:

> It was a sunny day and the sky was like a new sheet of blotting paper with the blue ink tipped into the middle of it.

What is achieved in this sentence, according to a Formalist analysis, is a transformation of the sentence 'The sky was blue' in such a way that one's flagging perceptions are chastened into a renewed attentiveness to the sky's blueness. The sentence does not serve a purely informative function; it focuses our attention on the image of the sky that is offered so as to heighten our perception of it as an aesthetic end in itself.

More at the level of content, the Formalists sought to reveal the devices through which the total structure of given works of literature might be said to defamiliarize, make strange or challenge certain dominant conceptions – ideologies even, although they did not use the word – of the social world. It is in this sense, for example, that the couplet Don Quixote/Sancho Panza might be said to figure as a device of 'defamiliarization' in relation to the canons of chivalric romance. Or, to give another example, it is clear that in Mark Twain's *The Adventures of*

Huckleberry Finn, Huck himself functions as a formal device whereby the ideological forms upholding the institution of slavery are turned inside out, made to appear strange and, in the process, called into question. Take the episode in which Huck and Jim, the escaped Negro slave who is his companion on the raft, come to the point in their journey down the Mississippi at which Cairo and, for Jim, freedom beckon:

> Jim talked out loud all the time while I was talking to myself. He was saying how the first thing he would do when he got to a free state he would go to saving up money and never spend a single cent, and when he got enough he would buy his wife, which was owned on a farm close to where Miss Watson lived; and then they would both work to buy the two children, and if their master wouldn't sell them, they'd get an Ab'litionist to go and steal them.
>
> It most froze me to hear such talk. He wouldn't ever dared to talk such talk in his life before. Just see what a difference it made in him the minute he judged he was about free. It was according to the old saying, 'give a nigger an inch and he'll take an ell.' Thinks I, this is what comes of my not thinking. Here was this nigger which I had as good as helped to run away, coming right out flat-footed and saying he would steal his children – children that belonged to a man I didn't even know; a man that hadn't ever done me no harm.[5]

The most interesting feature of this passage is the way in which the contortions of Huck's grammar reveal the contradiction between the reality of slavery and the ideological forms of individualism. What shocks Huck is not so much that Jim plans to buy or, if need be, steal his children from their owner, but the fact that Jim dares to imagine himself as the subject of any action whatever. Linguistically speaking, Jim constitutes himself as the subject of predication: he dares to imagine himself as an 'I' to whom there can be attributed an autonomous volition. He thinks and speaks for himself within language in anticipation of the situation in which he will be legally free to act for himself within the world. It is in a firm rebuttal of this that Huck refers to both Jim and his wife not as persons but as objects – 'his wife, which was owned on a farm'; 'this nigger which I had as good as helped to run away'. Slaves, Huck thus affirms, do not or should not think or act for themselves. They exist, linguistically, as objects within the discourse of others just as, economically, they are the property of others. In this linguistic tension – the tension between Jim as the 'I' of his own discourse and Jim as the 'which' of Huck's discourse – there is inscribed the tension between the ethical, political and linguistic imperatives of individualism and the limits to those imperatives as set by the institution of slavery, a tension which is made visible by the workings of the text.

Finally, and perhaps most sustainedly, the Formalists were concerned with the formal mechanisms whereby literary works tended to reveal or make strange the systems of coherence imposed on reality by the codes and conventions of other, usually earlier literary forms. Shklovsky's comments on Laurence Sterne's *Tristram Shandy* may be taken as typical in this respect.[6] Distinguishing between the concepts of *fabula* (or story) as the temporal-causal sequence of narrated events which comprise the raw materials of the work, and *sjuzet* (or plot) as the way in which these raw materials are formally manipulated, Shklovsky argues that the story of *Tristram Shandy* – ostensibly the life and opinions of Tristram – is told in such a way as to limit and reveal the narrative conventions of the time. According to these, the developing forms of novelistic realism purported to reflect the unfolding of events through an objective temporal sequence in which effect follows cause, cause begets effect and so on. By taking these conventions seriously and parodying them – by beginning at the beginning, with Tristram's conception – Sterne reveals their essentially formal and contrived nature in the innumerable digressions into which he is forced in order actually to locate a point in time which can be regarded as a beginning and, once located, to get beyond it. In this way, Sterne forces the conventions of novelistic realism into a corner where, their claim to be faithful and literal transcriptions of reality having been disavowed, they stand revealed as merely one set of formal conventions amongst others.

The influence of this latter concern on subsequent schools of literary criticism cannot be overestimated. It has provided both the inspiration and many of the concepts for the theories of Roland Barthes and, in this country, Stephen Heath, concerning the extent to which contemporary *avant-garde* literary practice – the works of James Joyce, Franz Kafka and, more recently, such exponents of the *nouveau roman* as

Alain Robbe-Grillet – can be viewed as enacting a work of transformation on the classical canons of novelistic realism.[7] These latter, they
argue, convey the illusion that they are literal transcriptions of reality,
forms in which, as it were, reality writes itself. In explicitly breaking
with, parodying or playing upon such conventions, contemporary
avant-garde literary practice is said to 'defamiliarize' such conventions: to
reveal them *as* conventions and, in so doing, to show how they condition our perceptions of reality by, precisely, refusing to conform to
them.

'The nouveau roman', as Stephen Heath puts it, '. . . is thus an essentially critical enterprise directed at a questioning of the assumptions
of the "Balzacian" novel and, through that, of the habitual forms in
which we define or *write* our lives.'[8] By refusing to end stories; by
beginning them at arbitrary points in time; by constantly re-running
the same sequence of events at different stages in the unfolding of the
narrative; by refusing any anthropomorphizing description of persons
or objects – in all of these ways, the practice of the *nouveau roman* reveals
the essentially social and conventional nature of those literary forms
which *do* construct their narrative universe in accordance with these
conventions.

To conclude this thumb-nail sketch of Formalism, then, the Formalists argued that literature should be regarded as a practice which,
through a variety of formal devices, enacts a transformation of received
categories of thought and expression. Subverting the particular patterns of thought or perception imposed on reality by the categories of
ordinary language, by dominant ideological forms or by the codes of
other literary works, literature is thus said to make such forms strange
and, in so doing, to weaken their grip on the ways in which we perceive the world. In this way, Shklovsky argued, literature 'creates a
"vision" of the object instead of serving as a means for knowing it'.[9] It
does not, as does science, organize the world conceptually, but rather
disorganizes the forms through which the world is customarily perceived,
opening up a kind of chink through which the world displays to view
new and unexpected aspects.

Finally, in all of this, the Formalists themselves had a strong preference for those literary forms which, rather than concealing or effacing
their own formal operations, explicitly display on their surface the

processes of their own working. This preference for the 'baring of the device' in part reflected their susceptibility to Kant's doctrine of art for art's sake. For, whereas realist modes of writing encourage the reader to read *through* the formal artistic devices, without noticing them, in order to appropriate the story that rests beneath them, those works which wear their formal operations on their sleeve force the reader to attend to the artistry of the work as an end in itself. Shklovsky was thus an outspoken supporter of *zaum* poetry which, by a deliberate play on words and their accepted meanings, aimed to produce a trans-rational language in which words functioned in a purely formal, artistic way.

REASSESSING FORMALISM

We can see from the above the sense in which, for the Formalists, it would have been inconceivable to regard any set of literary forms as being realistic in the sense that they somehow corresponded to reality itself. Formalism regards all literary forms as equally and necessarily *significations* of reality.[10] They differ merely with respect to the compendia of devices through which they effect their work of signification.

It was this perception that brought the Formalists into conflict with the developing schools of post-Revolutionary Marxist criticism which, especially in the 1920s, were increasingly dominated by the concerns of 'reflection theory'. This demanded that the relative merits of literary forms should be judged according to the extent to which they succeeded in accurately depicting or 'reflecting' the underlying logic and direction of historical development. From 1917 to 1923–4, partly because the Party had more pressing matters to attend to and partly because there was no clearly defined orthodoxy within Marxist criticism, the work of the Formalists was tolerated, even welcomed in some quarters. From the mid-1920s, however, they were subjected to increasing pressures to revise their negative estimation of the theory of reflection and to concern themselves with historical and sociological, as opposed to purely 'literary', considerations.

By 1929 these pressures, from being merely theoretical, had taken on a more bureaucratic and overtly political colour. Individual fates varied. Shklovsky and Eichenbaum remained in Russia where, by limiting their activities to routine textual criticism, they managed to survive the years of Stalinist repression. Jakobson migrated westward, eventually reaching Prague where he was to become the doyen of nascent Czech structuralism. But, by 1930, Formalism was effectively dead, and, by 1934, had become a mere synonym for the concepts of bourgeois decadence and escapism within the ideology of socialist realism promulgated by Zhdanov.

Putting the question of their political repression in the name of Zhdanovite orthodoxy to one side, it is still not easy to see how the concerns of the Russian Formalists might be squared with those of Marxist criticism. For, if there is a common core to Marxist criticism, it is the conviction that works of literature can be fully understood only if placed in the context of the economic, social and political relationships in which they are produced. The Formalists, by contrast, *tended* to insist on the autonomy of literature, regarding the proper business of criticism as being solely with the analysis of the formal properties of literary texts. Similarly, whereas Marxism adopts a political stance in relation to literature, imputing certain political effects to works of literature and seeking to evaluate those effects from its own political position, the Formalists *tended* to be apolitical in their approach, viewing the aesthetic effect of defamiliarization to which works of literature were said to give rise as an end in itself, divorced from political considerations or consequences.

The difficulty of conducting a dialogue between Formalist and Marxist criticism has been compounded by the circumstances in which the work of the Formalists first entered into critical debate in the west. Although Brecht was influenced by Formalist ideas in developing his theory of epic theatre,[11] the Formalists seem not to have had any appreciable impact on literary scholarship in the West until the publication, in 1955, of Victor Erlich's *Russian Formalism – History, Doctrine*, and, in 1965, of Tzvetan Todorov's *Textes des Formalistes Russes*. As both of these appeared contemporaneously with and assisted in the emergence of structuralism and semiotics as influential perspectives within the study of literature, both tended to stress the continuities between Formalism and contemporary structuralist criticism. The accuracy of this assessment will concern us shortly. Meanwhile, so far as any *rapprochement* with Marxism is concerned, this particular form of the 'rediscovery' of the Formalists has been unfortunate. For, apart from a period of brief flirtation in the early 1960s, Marxists have come to regard structuralism as a new idealism, indeed a new 'formalism', with the result that the Formalists have often been condemned as guilty by mere association.

It is only recently that a sustained dialogue between Formalism and Marxism has become possible. This is not to say that such a dialogue has not previously been called for. 'Every young science', Pavel Medvedev wrote, with the Formalists in mind, '– and Marxist literary scholarship is very young – must much more highly prize a good foe than a poor ally.'[12] This was in the late 1920s when Medvedev, together with his companion critic Mikhail Bakhtin and the linguist Valentin Vološinov (arguably the same person), was himself engaged in such a dialogue which, however, was curtailed by the same political pressures which dispersed the Formalists. More recently, Roland Barthes has admonished that, had it been 'less terrorized by the spectre of "formalism", historical criticism might have been less sterile'.[13]

These are exceptions, however, and for the greater part of the Left the most influential commentary on the Formalists has been that offered by Trotsky. Yet, although not entirely unsympathetic to the Formalists, Trotsky's overall assessment of their work was significantly off-centre. It was methodologically unsound in that it judged the Formalists solely on the basis of Shklovsky's polemical early writings which were not at all representative of the actual accomplishments of Formalism. It was, furthermore, contradictory. In seeking to distance himself from the charge of economic reductionism, Trotsky accepted, with qualifications, the Formalist thesis that artistic creation effects 'a deflection, a changing and a transformation of reality, in accordance with the peculiar laws of art'.[14] Yet he also criticized the Formalists for concerning themselves overmuch with the minutiae of poetic devices in spite of their claim that it was only by studying these that the precise nature of the transformation to which works of art subject reality could be fully understood. Although willing to adopt the phraseology of the Formalists concerning the relative autonomy of art, Trotsky at the same time belittled the concrete empirical work which could alone transform that phraseology from empty slogan-mongering into a sustained theoretical position.

In spite of this central contradiction, Trotsky's work has been responsible for the spread of a stereotype of the Russian Formalists as humble 'underlabourers of the device' who, concerned solely with the minutiae of literary forms, are alleged to have dismissed social and historical considerations as irrelevant. It will accordingly repay our attention to show that, in the actual conduct of their criticism, the Formalists were not so apolitical, ahistorical or asociological, so 'formalist', as the stereotype would have us believe.

HISTORICAL PERSPECTIVES ON RUSSIAN FORMALISM

Although the Bolshevik Party faced more pressing problems of an economic, political and military nature after the Revolution, it was also faced with the need to develop a policy in the artistic sphere. Unfortunately, there existed no well-developed body of theory in relation to which such a policy might be developed. The result, in the absence of an authoritative theoretical voice at the political centre, was a complex concatenation of divergent voices competing with one another for Party approval.

This is not the place for a detailed consideration of these matters.[15] Suffice it to say that the most influential of the competing literary-political tendencies were, first, the Proletkult and its later offshoots, notably the Russian Association of Proletarian Writers. Heir to the populist tradition of Russian criticism, the Proletkult valued chiefly the agitational value of a militantly proletarian revolutionary literature – that is, of literature which depicted the barriers to socialism being overthrown by the revolutionary will of its central, largely working-class, protagonists. Second, there were those, notably Maxim Gorky, who supported the value of traditional realism and the role of the 'fellow travellers'. Arguing that literature had a cognitive function, offering a knowledge of historical development through an anthropomorphic and poetically concrete depiction of the socially typical, they argued that revolutionary literature should aim to reflect historical contradictions and not to conjure them away through an excess of revolutionary optimism. It was this position that was nearest to Party orthodoxy and which, in the 1930s, was taken up, extended and developed by Georg Lukács.

Finally, there were the Futurists who aimed to revolutionize literature not by revolutionizing its content but by revolutionizing the techniques of literary production. They sought to use literature to promote neither a substitute for scientific knowledge, nor revolutionary sentiment, but the shock effect of recognition, inducing a new perception of reality by modifying the forms through which it is customarily perceived.

The position of the Formalists amidst this array of competing voices varied from individual to individual and changed as the climate of criticism itself changed. They did not, however, attempt to debate *politically* with the Revolution. Far from being linked with reactionary social forces, they were amongst the first group of intellectuals to declare their support for the new regime. They were more ambivalent, however, with regard to the theoretical and political debates about literature unleashed by the Revolution. Whilst, prior to 1920, the Formalists sought to maintain a critical distance from these controversies, this aloofness proved impossible in the 1920s. Drawn inexorably into the maelstrom of debate, their position changed significantly.

The critical factor in this development was the Formalists' relationship to Futurism. It would be mistaken to view Formalism as the theory of which Futurism was the practice. But there was undoubtedly a close connection between the two. At the theoretical level, the Futurists' politically motivated concern to disrupt habitualized ways of seeing bore a close relationship to the Formalists' more general theoretical concern with the devices whereby literary works attained their effect of defamiliarization. The work of the Futurists thus formed a convenient illustration of the Formalists' central thesis and was often quoted with approval by them.[16] These theoretical connections were consolidated at a personal level, chiefly through Mayakovsky. The leading exponent and theorist of Futurism, the editor of the Futurist journals *Lef* and *Novy Lef*, Mayakovsky also participated in the affairs of the Moscow Linguistic Circle and *Opoyaz*, thus ensuring an active exchange of ideas between the two movements.

It was largely as a result of this connection with the Futurists that the Formalists were induced to revise their contention that the literary device was 'unmotivated' and to take more seriously the claims of social and historical considerations in literary scholarship. The Formalists, as we have seen, initially subscribed to a form of 'art for art's sake'. As Shklovsky put it:

> The technique of art is to make objects 'unfamiliar', to make forms difficult, to increase the difficulty and length of perception because the process of perception is an aesthetic end in itself and must be prolonged.[17]

Shklovsky thus viewed the literary device as being 'unmotivated'. The defamiliarization to which it gives rise, that is, was not thought to be motivated by any consideration beyond that of promoting a renewed and sharpened attentiveness to reality. The category of defamiliarization was thus invested with a purely aesthetic, and not with an ideological significance.

This ran quite contrary to the position of the Futurists who viewed the devices of defamiliarization as a means for promoting political awareness by undermining ideologically habituated modes of perception. As Osip Brik summarized the Futurists' position:

> Thus art was still 'a device'; what had changed from the original Formalist interpretation was the application of the device. The emphasis was shifted from the aesthetic function of the device to its use in the service of a 'social demand'. All the manifestations of the device, including the extreme case of 'the device laid bare' in trans-sense poetry, were now considered in the light of their potential social utility: '*not an aesthetic end in itself, but a laboratory for the best possible expression of the facts of the present day.*'[18]

However, although the Formalists accepted the Kantian thesis of 'art for art's sake', they did not regard this, as do most idealist aesthetic theorists, as the product of some invariant aesthetic faculty rooted in the human psyche. They rather viewed the essentially self-referring nature of literary works as a product of the objective properties of such works. This was particularly the case in the Formalists' writings on poetry where it was argued that, through the mechanisms of what Mukařovský was later to call 'foregrounding', the poetic word functioned so as to signify merely itself and its own usage and not any content beyond itself, 'to place in the foreground the act of expression, the act of speech itself'.[19]

'Art for art's sake', then, was understood in a specifically materialist sense as the product of objective formal devices which were fully amenable to scientific analysis. However, even this conception was modified in the light of the theoretical demands placed on the Formalists by the Futurists.

The role of *Lef* and, later, *Novy Lef* was crucial in this respect. Attempting, on the one hand, to persuade revolutionary artists not to underrate the contribution of the Formalists, these journals simultaneously called upon the Formalists to enhance the value of their contribution by providing a sociohistorical, as opposed to purely technical, account of literary devices together with an analysis of the ideological motivations which accounted for the use to which such devices were put.[20]

There is no doubt that the Formalists responded to these demands. In part, this resulted in a re-examination of the Kantian premises on which their earlier writings had rested, but, more sustainedly, it also led to greater appreciation of the relevance of historical and sociological considerations to the concerns of literary scholarship.

This is a matter on which the Formalists have been perhaps most persistently misunderstood. Jakobson, seeking retrospectively to set the record straight, wrote:

> Neither Tynyanov, nor Mukařovský, nor Shklovsky, nor I have preached that art is sufficient unto itself; on the contrary, we show that art is a part of the social edifice, a component correlating with the others, a variable component, since the sphere of art and its relationship with other sectors of the social structure ceaselessly changes dialectically. What we stress is not a separation of art, but the autonomy of the aesthetic function.[21]

Jakobson relies on the wisdom of hindsight a little too much here. For the Formalists – especially Shklovsky – were not always so clear about the nature of their concerns as this would imply.[22] Nevertheless, it is true to say that, for the greater part, the Formalists did not maintain that works of literature existed in an ahistorical vacuum. They merely argued that the organizational features which distinguished such works as precisely works of 'literature' could not be reduced to economic, social or historical considerations. There was therefore a need, they claimed, for an autonomous level of theorizing, concerned solely with the formal properties of literary texts, if those features which uniquely distinguished literary works were to be properly understood. It was only in relation to this facet of literary texts – their literariness – and not in relation to such texts as totalities that the Formalists maintained that social and historical considerations were irrelevant.

Where they were on perhaps more shaky ground was in their attempt to explain the dynamics of literary evolution as entirely the result of developmental tendencies at work within literature itself. It was in relation to this issue, and not the question of literariness, that the Formalists conceded ground in the direction of history and sociology. There is no doubt that, in part, these concessions were merely cynical responses to political necessity. Surveying the variety of syntheses between Formalism, history and sociology proposed by the Formalists in the mid-1920s, Victor Erlich concludes that they were, for the most part, merely mechanical, a synthesis of slogans and not of theoretical perspectives.[23]

Nevertheless, the need to take account of social and historical considerations was prompted as much by theoretical as by political necessity. At root, the Formalists contended that literary forms tended to change and develop simply as a result of the passage of time itself. New literary forms are called into being, they argued, by the need to challenge and disrupt those forms and conventions, innovative and de-familiarizing in their own day, whose cutting edge has been dulled through overuse. Yet it was made increasingly clear, particularly by the pace and extremely radical nature of literary experimentation in post-Revolutionary Russia, that neither the tempo nor the direction of literary change could be explained in this way.

Jurij Tynyanov's and Roman Jakobson's essay on 'Problems in the Study of Literature and Language' (1927) is widely regarded as a critical turning point in this respect. Although the autonomy of literature is still insisted upon, that autonomy is now conceived as relative in nature. Tynyanov and Jakobson formally acknowledge that the history of literature could only be written by relating it to the histories governing the development of economic, social and political relationships. Whilst each of these levels of social activity is regarded as being autonomous in relation to the others in the sense that each is governed by quite specific and irreducible laws, Tynyanov and Jakobson contend that they are also inextricably interconnected and can only be explained with reference to the interaction between them within the 'system of systems' constituted by the concrete historical society concerned:

> The history of literature (art), being simultaneous with other historical series, is characterized, as is each of these series, by an involved complex of structural laws. Without an elucidation of these laws, it is impossible to establish in a scientific manner the correlation between the literary series and other historical series. . . . However, these laws do not allow us to explain the tempo of evolution or the chosen path of evolution when several, theoretically possible, evolutionary paths are given. This is owing to the fact that the immanent laws of literary (linguistic) evolution form an indeterminate equation; although they admit only a limited number of possible solutions, they do not necessarily specify a unique solution. The question of the specific choice of path, or at least of the dominant, can be solved only by means of the correlation between the literary series and the other historical series. This correlation (a system of systems) has its own structural laws, which must be submitted to investigation.[24]

This text is frequently interpreted as having marked the foundations of structuralism. Such a reading is strictly retrospective, motivated more by Jakobson's subsequent association with Czech structuralism than by the theoretical position outlined in the text itself. For the structuralist usually maintains not merely that the various levels of human activity should be regarded as relatively autonomous. He also contends that, as there is present in each of these an order of culture, each should be viewed as being organized like a language. Perhaps one of the more famous and extreme examples of this position is Claude Lévi-Strauss' argument – aptly summarized in his contention that incest is 'bad grammar' – that kinship systems can be viewed as systems of rules regulating the exchange of women and goods which, in their structure, conform to the model of a language.[25]

Tynyanov and Jakobson do not take this step of assuming that the methods involved in the study of language can be directly transferred to the study of other areas of social and cultural activity. Indeed, in suggesting that the correlation between systems 'has its own structural laws, which must be submitted to investigation', they explicitly go *beyond* structuralism, which has so far proved notoriously incapable of proposing a theoretical framework within which such questions might be posed.[26]

Furthermore, in certain respects, their position anticipates the concerns of contemporary Marxism as defined by Louis Althusser.[27] For Althusser, too, conceives of society or, more accurately, a 'social formation', as consisting of a number of relatively autonomous 'instances' or levels of social practice – the economic, the political and the ideological. And he has further argued that the essential concern of Marxism is to understand the ways in which these levels of practice interact with one another within concrete historical societies. In doing so, he has opened up a new set of concerns within Marxism, a new way of looking at problems that, in its implications for Marxist criticism, suggests close parallels with the concerns of the Formalists.

NEW DIRECTIONS IN MARXIST CRITICISM

It is surprising, in the light of this brief historical resumé, that the Russian Formalists should have been so neglected by Western Marxists. The explanation is in part political. The debate about literature within Western Communist Parties has, until recently, reflected the terms of the debate within Russia which, as the world's first socialist state, enjoyed enormous prestige and authority in the West, not to mention the more tangible powers of direction assumed by the Comintern. In Germany, the intellectual centre of European Marxism in the 1920s and 1930s, the weight of Soviet orthodoxy was relayed to the German movement via the debates conducted within the *Bund des Proletarisches Revolutionärer Schriftstellers* (BPRS) – the Association of Revolutionary Proletarian Writers. It was, in view of this, no accident that the dispersal of the Formalists and Futurists coincided, in Germany, with the defeat of Expressionism within the affairs of the BPRS and the consolidation of 'the Lukács line', a highly sophisticated version of Soviet critical orthodoxy which, if it was not a dogma, quite clearly specified the terms within which the debate was henceforward to be conducted.[28]

Not by politics alone, however. Theoretical considerations also have their own determinations and effects, and it was the theoretical and philosophical assumptions of the Lukácsian approach to literature which most effectively impeded the possibility of any fruitful dialogue between Formalist and Marxist criticism. We might usefully single out two matters for consideration here.

The first concerns the impact of Hegelian categories of thought on Marxist aesthetics during this period. Partly as a result of Lukács' own work and, allied with this, the influence of Marx's *Economic and Philosophical Manuscripts*, first published in 1931, Western Marxism was, from the 1930s through to the 1960s, dominated by the influence of Hegel. The consequence of this, in the aesthetic sphere, was the devaluation of considerations of form in relation to those of content. Hegel had argued that the sensuous, material forms of works of art were but the external, more or less contingent manifestations of the philosophical contents they were said to contain and express. In a similar vein, the dominant concern of Marxist criticism during this period was with the social determination of the philosophical content of literary works. Specifically formal questions – in the sense understood by the Formalists – virtually disappeared from discussion as the concept of form was reinterpreted so as to refer not to the distinctive narrative structure of the literary text but to the structure of the 'world view' which was said to inform its social vision.

In Lukács' view, for example, the most important questions about Tolstoy's works had little to do with the place of their narrative techniques within the history of writing. Rather, Lukács was concerned with the respects in which the social vision they contained could be taken to express the world view of the Russian peasantry. In this connection, the formal distinctions between Tolstoy's literary and his theological or philosophical writings were regarded as being of no importance whatsoever.[29] These were regarded as purely 'surface' differences; what mattered was the essential unity of content, of social and philosophical world view, that was alleged to exist beneath them. In short: the conduct of Marxist criticism during this period was such that the formal differences between different types of writing – literary, poetic, theological, philosophical – was overlooked in pursuit of the similar philosophical contents that could be discovered within and abstracted from them.

The second matter has to do with the extent to which the notion of literature as a form of signifying practice was replaced by a concern with literature as a form of 'reflection'. According to 'reflection theory', the crucial question refers not to the precise ways in which, in the light of their formal properties, works of literature *signify* reality but rather to the extent of their correspondence to it. It was, again, Lukács who revived the full thrust of the Aristotelian concept of mimesis according to which the literary work is regarded as pushing beyond the world of surface appearances to capture, crystallize and reflect 'the essence of things'. The necessary corollary of such a concern was an attempt to rank literary forms according to the degree to which they corresponded to 'the essence of things' – in this case, the class struggle as 'already known' within the terms of Marxist theory. True, literature was still regarded as a particular type of knowledge, working via devices of typification so as to yield an anthropomorphic, poetically concrete representation of the dynamic tendencies of historical development. However, it was evaluated not in terms of the effects of its distinctive organizational properties but in terms of the degree of its correspondence to the model of reality proposed by Marxism.

It was, then, a combination of political and theoretical determinations which precluded any meaningful dialogue between Formalism and Marxism. If such a dialogue is now possible, this is mainly due to the theoretical reorientations which have taken place, since the 1960s, within Marxist criticism itself. Many influences have been at work here. Most important, from our point of view, is the pivotal position which the work of Louis Althusser has assumed in relation to the revision of Marxist criticism which is currently in progress. To understand the respects in which this is so, a schematic account of Althusser's reading of Marxism is called for. The distinction he proposes between two different ways of conceiving the nature of the social totality is particularly relevant to our purposes here. For these have markedly different implications for the way in which the concerns of Marxist criticism should be approached.

In opposing Hegelian interpretations of Marxism, especially as represented by Lukács, Althusser refers to the Hegelian conception of the social totality as an 'expressive totality'. It represents the social whole as a totality whose parts are conceived as 'so many "*total parts*", each expressing the others, and each expressing the social totality that contains them, because each in itself contains in the immediate form of its expression the essence of the social totality itself.'[30] The essence of the social totality, according to Hegelian versions of Marxism, is said to be defined by the essential contradiction which is at its centre. This is usually construed as the clash between the dynamic momentum of new forces of economic production and the restraining hand of old social relations of production. This essential contradiction is then said to be present in, and therefore capable of being deduced or read off from, each of the constituent parts which, taken together, comprise the social totality. We find such a conception of the social totality deeply ingrained in Lukács' literary criticism which, at root, treats literary texts as privileged forms of consciousness which can be read so as to reveal the essential contradiction of the historical period to which they refer.

Althusser, by contrast, argues that the social totality should not be regarded as being governed by a simple or essential contradiction. Instead, he contends, it should be viewed as consisting of a number of distinct but inter-related 'instances' or levels of practical activity – the *economic*, the *political*, the *ideological* – each of which is relatively autonomous in relation to the others in the sense that it is governed by laws of its own that cannot be read off from elsewhere and each of which possesses its own relative effectivity in relation to the others. Change, according to such a formulation, results not from the working out of a basic or simple contradiction – such as that between the forces and relations of production – but from the overlapping, in a particular historical conjuncture, of a number of distinct, relatively autonomous contradictions. Change occurs when the contradictions which are unique to the *ideological* level of social practice overlap and combine with those which are unique to the *economic* and *political* levels of social practice, yielding a situation in which contradiction is thus said to be 'overdetermined'.

The central problem which has had to be tackled in order to sustain this formulation has thus been to determine precisely what distinguishes each of these levels of social practice and to analyse the nature of their interaction in concrete historical societies. In the case of literature, this has meant that any analysis which sets out to read literary texts so as to reveal the essence of the social whole to which they refer must prove irrelevant. Another sort of analysis is required which attempts to reveal the precise nature of literature's specific difference with reference to other ideological or cultural forms and to articulate the precise place it occupies in relation to the other levels of social practice which, together with it, comprise the social totality. Furthermore, rather than the concern being with how literature 'reflects' social reality, attention is focused on the effects which it is possible to attribute to literature as an autonomous level of social practice. Thus, literature is viewed, not as a secondary reflection of something else, but as a real social force, existing in its own right, with its own determinations and effects.

The result of this reorientation has been to bring the question of the specific nature of literature, as a particular type of signifying practice, firmly back into the centre of discussion. If literature is to be regarded as an autonomous level of social practice and, as such, is to be made the object of an autonomous level of theorizing within Marxism, then clearly the question of specifying the features which uniquely distinguish works of literature from other ideological and cultural forms becomes a matter of prime importance.

But it was precisely this problem which faced the Formalists. If there is ever to develop a truly scientific study of literature, they argued, then such a science must first specify its object – it must, that is, provide a definition for the concept of 'literature'. Hence their enduring concern with the problem of literariness. Nor do the similarities between Althusser and the Formalists end here. The two positions closely resemble one another in respect of the processes by which they construct the concepts of literature with which they work. Furthermore, the definitions which they propose for the concept of literature have much in common. Althusser, for example, has argued that the specific nature of literature consists in the transformations to which it subjects the categories of dominant ideology, distancing them from within, providing a 'vision' of them at work so that, within the literary work, the reader is to an extent divorced from the habitual mental associations which the forms of dominant ideology foster. Similarly, the Formalists contended that the uniqueness of literary discourse consisted in the work of transformation it enacts on ordinary language – the primal home of all ideology – by subverting the conventional relationship between signifier and signified so as to restore a new perceptibility to the world.

However, we will not dwell on these similarities here. There are equally important differences between the two positions. It is not our intention to argue that the theories developed from within these two traditions are identical but merely that they occupy sufficient common ground for their juxtaposition to be fruitful. For whilst both occupy the familiar terrain of traditional aesthetics in proposing a theory of 'literature' as such, they both tend to undermine that terrain and, in so doing, to call into question the concept of 'literature' as an irrevocably separate form of writing which is sealed off from other forms of cultural practice by some universal and invariant set of formal properties.

3

RUSSIAN FORMALISM: CLEARING THE GROUND

LINGUISTICS AND LITERATURE

My concern in this chapter is to probe some of the issues already raised a little more closely; to move a little closer to some of the central concepts of the Formalists in order to locate the theoretical, philosophical and methodological bedrock which gave a thematic coherence to their diverse critical concerns. It will be convenient to treat Ferdinand de Saussure's work as the pivot on which to centre our discussion. For, of the many influences which coalesced in the formation of Russian Formalism, that exerted by Saussure and by linguistics in general was arguably of primary importance.

It is important, however, to be clear about the different levels at which this influence operated. The argument which maintains that there is an uninterrupted line of development running from Saussurian linguistics through Formalism to present-day structuralism hinges on the relationship between the methodologies of these three traditions. Saussure's central methodological perception was that the value and function of a given unit of language, its accepted meaning, depends on its relationship to other such units within the system of language. His recommendation was that the study of this system of relationships

– *la langue* – should be the proper concern of linguistics. The structural-ist projection consists, essentially, in the contention that cultural forms – such as myths, folk tales, literature – can themselves be viewed as being articulated like a language and that methods of study derived from linguistics should accordingly be used in their analysis.

To the extent that the Formalists did argue that the value and func-tion of a literary device depends on its relationship to other devices within the system of relationships established by the literary text as a whole, it is quite correct to point to their influence on the formation of structuralism. But the argument has its limits, chiefly because it depends considerably on the work of Jakobson which was atypical of that of Formalism as a whole.

For Jakobson was interested in literature as merely one area amongst others – notably folklore – to which the developing methods of lin-guistics might be applied. Although he was careful to note that the techniques of linguistics should not be directly transferred, without modification, to the study of literature – meaning, here, the *belles lettres* of the European tradition – in the respect that the latter was, unlike languages or folk tales, a typically individual as opposed to a collective, anonymous creation, the strength of the linguistic connection did significantly modify his approach to literature.[1] This is particularly clear in his writings on poetry, especially during the period of his association with Czech structuralism. Poetry became, for Jakobson, the manifestation of a particular set of linguistic operations which, by setting the poetic word free from the normal associations which define and restrict its meaning in prosaic speech, served to call attention to the act of communication itself. Poetry, on this definition, is the self-consciousness of language. It consists of those forms through which language offers its own mechanisms and workings conspicuously to view.

The inevitable consequence of this view was to push poetics and, more generally, the study of literature back into the study of language, to make it a specialized province within the general science of lin-guistics. This ran entirely contrary to the interests and motivation of the members of *Opoyaz* whose primary concern, as we have seen, was that the study of literature should be constituted as a genuinely autonomous science, employing distinctive methods and procedures of its own, and not as a part of some other science, even that of linguistics. Although undoubtedly influenced by linguistics, they did not take the structuralist step of assuming that literature was a system *like* language. To the contrary, they argued that literature was not a work *of* language but a work *on* language, an autonomous practice whose uniqueness consisted, amongst other things, in the transformations to which it subjected the categories of ordinary language.

Paradoxically, in thus distancing themselves from linguistics, the Formalists were merely following through the implications of their philosophical conception of the relationship that exists between a science and its object – in their case, the object of literariness – which was, at root, not dissimilar to that put forward by Saussure.

THE QUESTION OF LITERARINESS: CRITICISM AND ITS OBJECT

It has already been pointed out that the ultimate concern of the Formalists was with the concept of literariness. They approached particular literary texts not as ends in themselves, to be understood on their own terms and for their own sake, but as vehicles for the exemplification and development of this concept. To appreciate more deeply what was involved in such a concern, it will be helpful to review the problems which confronted Saussure and the means by which he resolved them.

Surveying the history of linguistics toward the end of the nineteenth century, Saussure contended that it had failed to establish the study of language on a scientific footing chiefly because it had 'never attempted to determine the nature of its object'. For, he argued, 'without this elementary operation a science cannot develop an appropriate method'.[2] Whereas in empiricist theories of knowledge science is held to furnish a knowledge of an object or reality which is held to exist independently of its own conceptual procedures, Saussure argued that, in science, 'far from it being the object that antedates the viewpoint, it would seem that it is the viewpoint that creates the object'.[3]

Saussure thus contended that it would be impossible to found linguistics on a scientific basis if its concerns were taken to be with all aspects of language as a presumed real entity existing externally to and independently of scientific thought about it. If progress were to be made, he argued, the science of linguistics must specify those aspects of language it would make the object of its inquiry: it must construct an artificial conceptual or theoretical object out of the heterogeneity of language and limit its investigations to the conceptual field thus specified. He therefore proposed a distinction between the concept of *la parole* – individual speech utterances – and *la langue* – the system of rules which, governing the permissible forms of combination of the units of language, make the production and communication of meaning in individual speech utterances possible – and argued that linguistics should concern itself exclusively with *la langue*.

This distinction is, of course, a purely methodological one. *La parole* and *la langue* are not, in reality, either separate or separable from one another. The knowledge which linguistics was thus to produce was not a knowledge of the 'real' nature of language but a knowledge of the conceptual object of *la langue*, an object of science's own making. The relationship of 'knowledge' between a science and its object was thus, so far as Saussure was concerned, located entirely within thought itself.

The Formalists faced similar problems with reference to the study of literature. Surveying the schools of criticism available to them, they argued that their crucial deficiency was their tendency to dissolve the study of literature into the study of something else – biography, the history of ideas, sociology or psychoanalysis – as the study of a particular text was pushed back into a study of its author's personal history, his intellectual and social milieu or his unconsciousness. What was missing, they argued, was a concern with the literary text itself and with the principles governing its construction as a particular type of discourse. This meant that the study of literature, rather than resting on any autonomous body of theory, was forced into dependency on the theories and methods of those continents of knowledge – be they those of psychoanalysis, sociology or linguistics – to which the text was referred.

If there was a rallying cry which united the Formalists, it was that the study of literature should become an autonomous science, putting to work methods and procedures of its own. For this to be possible, such a science would need first to specify the nature of the object to which it would address itself, to state clearly what it was to be a science of and to map out clearly the conceptual space it would occupy. This

boiled down, as we have seen, to the question of literariness: of determining the precise nature of literature's uniqueness and of developing
the appropriate theoretical concepts and methodological procedures to
analyse the formal properties which conferred on literary texts their
uniqueness.

Behind this concern was the perception that the concept of 'literature' would need to be spelt out with some degree of rigour and
precision if literary criticism were to advance beyond drawing room
chitchat and make serious claims to scholarship. In recognizing that the
construction of the object (or set of concerns) to which criticism
should address itself was a primary and indispensable *theoretical* process,
the Formalists thus took direct issue with the empiricist assumption,
discussed earlier, that literature exists as an external datum which is
simply 'given' to criticism. The 'literature' to which the Formalists
addressed themselves was not simply 'already there'; it was a product
of their own conceptual labours, a particular way of viewing so-called
'literary' texts which reflected a specific set of theoretical choices. In
this way, Formalist criticism produced its own *problematic*: that is, its
own set of problems and its own way of approaching those problems.

It is important to be clear about this. For, at one level, the Formalists
could be said to have aimed simply at providing a working definition
for the concept of 'literature' so that, in using this to sift out 'literary'
from 'non-literary' texts, the field of inquiry might be circumscribed.
Whilst this is partly true, the concept of literariness had the further
function of specifying *the actual object of inquiry itself*. Jakobson was
quite explicit on this. 'The real field of literary science', he wrote in
1919, 'is not literature but *literariness*; in other words, that which makes
a specific work literary.'[4] The specific object of literary criticism is thus
not the full plenitude of the literary text as something that is simply
pre-given to criticism but that specific aspect of the literary text which
makes it different from the non-literary series of cultural forms which
surround it.

As we have seen, the Formalists argued that this difference consisted
in the tendency of literary works to defamiliarize experience by working on and transforming the adjacent ideological and cultural forms
within which reality is dominantly experienced. The prime task for
literary criticism became that of analysing the constructional devices

whereby this effect of defamiliarization was achieved. The object of the Formalists' research was thus not the concrete object of literary texts themselves but the *abstract object of the differential relation between literary texts and non-literary texts*, a problematic (in the sense defined above) that was entirely the product of their own theoretical procedures.

The paradox at the heart of the Formalists' endeavour was that the more they pursued this object, the more it receded from view. For they were forced, by the logic of their own researches, to call into question the assumption that there existed a fixed and stable body of texts which might be regarded as 'literature'. In Formalist parlance, the question as to whether a given text should be described as 'literary' could be resolved only with reference to the function it fulfilled. And that, so it turned out, obliged the Formalists to take account of considerations that were inescapably and radically historical.

THE SYSTEM AND ITS ELEMENTS: FORM AND FUNCTION

It is often argued that the Formalists viewed literary texts in a vacuum, regarding their 'literariness' – their ability to 'defamiliarize' – as an attribute of their purely formal, intrinsic properties. To gainsay this, one must keep in mind the inherently *relational* nature of the concept of defamiliarization. To study the phenomenon of literariness is to study the relationship between the series of texts designated as 'literary' and those 'non-literary' (but linguistic) cultural forms which literary texts transform by 'making strange' the terms of seeing proposed in them. Whether or not a given text can be said to embody the attribute of defamiliarization thus depends not on its *intrinsic* properties in isolation but on the *relationship* which those properties establish with other cultural and ideological forms.

The accusation that the Formalists tended to fetishize the literary device is similarly misconceived. For the effect of defamiliarization depends not on the device itself but on the use to which it is put. 'The evidence of art itself', Eichenbaum suggests, 'is that its *differentia specifica* is not expressed in the elements that go to make up the individual work but simply in the particular use that is made of them.'[5] Literary language is distinguished from prosaic language, for example, not by the presence of metaphors in the former and their absence from the latter, but by the different use to which the device of metaphor is put as between the two cases. Erlich argues:

> If in informative prose, a metaphor aims to bring the subject closer to the audience or drive a point home, in 'poetry' it serves as a means of intensifying the intended aesthetic effect. Rather than translating the unfamiliar into the terms of the familiar, the poetic image 'makes strange' the habitual by presenting it in a novel light, by placing it in an unexpected context.[6]

In this, the Formalists were again following Saussure in the distinction he maintained between the synchronic and diachronic levels of analysis – that is, between the analysis of language as a static system of rules as it exists at any one point in time and the analysis of its historical change and development. In designating *la langue* as the proper object of linguistics, Saussure's concern was with the system of arbitrary conventions regulating the relationships between signifiers (such as 'ox') and their signifieds ('the concept of an ox') which make the production of meaning possible within a given language community. Historical considerations, he argued, were irrelevant to this task. For the meaning of a given unit of language can only be derived from an analysis of its place and function in relation to the other elements of *la langue* and is unaffected by considerations relating to its philological source or historical genesis. The word 'ox', for example, derives its meaning from the present synchronic relationships of similarity and difference which exist between its sound structure and that of other words comprising modern English, and not from whatever roots it might have in Old Norse, Anglo-Saxon or medieval French.

Insisting on a similar synchronic/diachronic polarity, the Formalists concerned themselves not so much with the origins of literary devices as with their mode of functioning in particular texts. 'The study of literary genetics', as Eichenbaum put it, 'can clarify only the origin of a device, nothing more; poetics must explain its literary function.'[7] The same device, then, may serve different functions in different literary texts. The central device of the mystery novel whereby the identity of the murderer is concealed from the reader may play a quite humdrum, purely technical role as in Agatha Christie's works. Alternatively, it may, by being used differently, figure as a device by which the conventions of the conventional detective story are 'made strange'.

Robbe-Grillet's *The Voyeur* provides an example of this as the travelling salesman, Mathias, constantly stumbles, like an unwitting sleuth, over the traces of the crime he has himself committed. (Or has he? Is it all just imaginings? – Robbe-Grillet leaves these questions permanently unanswered.) In thus doubling as the reader of signs (the sleuth) and their author (the murderer who has left behind the signs of his crime), Mathias serves to call into question the fixed division of labour between writer and reader which the traditional novel proposes. In figuring, as it were, as the reader of his own story, Mathias offers to view the conventions whereby the relationship between the roles of writer (the issuing source of meaning) and reader (the passive recipient of the offered meaning) is constructed in realist forms.

The concept by means of which the Formalists thought through this notion of the variability of the function of the device was that of 'the dominant'. This, as Seldon describes it, constitutes 'that focusing component of a work which governs and orders other components and guarantees the integrity of the entire structure.'[8] Although forming an important part of their theory of literary evolution, the concept is also important to an understanding of the Formalists' central concept of *ostranenie* or defamiliarization as 'the dominant' which specifies the function of the device within the uniquely literary work.

To appreciate why, we must first be clear about the relationship which is held to exist between those texts which are said to embody this attribute and reality. It is important to distinguish the position of the Formalists from that of the Futurists on this matter. As with most new literary tendencies, the Futurists proclaimed that their techniques wrested reality away from its deformation in older literary forms to reveal it in its raw state, its pristine purity. 'If fact is needed,' *Novy Lef* proclaimed, 'old art is no use. Old art deforms facts – to grasp facts use new methods.'[9] However, as Jakobson brilliantly maintained in his essay 'On Realism in Art', all literary forms are equally conventional modes of signifying reality no matter what ideological claims they might lodge with respect to their 'realism'. In contradistinction to the Futurists, the defamiliarization effected by literary texts does not, according to the Formalists, reveal the world 'as it really is' but merely constitutes one distinctive form of cognition amongst others.

Shklovsky makes this clear in the distinction he proposes between 'recognition' and 'seeing':

> This new attitude to objects in which, in the last analysis, the object becomes perceptible, is that artificiality which, in our opinion, creates art. A phenomenon, perceived many times, and no longer perceivable, or rather, the method of such dimmed perception, is what I call 'recognition' as opposed to 'seeing'. The aim of imagery, the aim of creating new art is to return the object from 'recognition' to 'seeing'.[10]

Literature is thus distinguishable as one among several different forms of cognition. In particular, it is distinguished from the way in which reality is spontaneously experienced in prosaic language and from the abstractions of science. It offers neither a direct, experiential relation to reality nor a scientific knowledge of it, but a 'vision' of it.

Likewise, the 'reality' which literary works are said to defamiliarize is not some presumed raw, conceptually unprocessed, 'out-there' reality but 'reality' as mediated through the categories of some other form of cognition. Literature characteristically works on and subverts those linguistic, perceptual and cognitive forms which conventionally condition our access to 'reality' and which, in their taken-for-grantedness, present the particular 'reality' they construct as *reality* itself. Literature thus effects a two-fold shift of perceptions. For what it makes appear strange is not merely the 'reality' which has been distanced from habitual modes of representation but also those habitual modes of representation themselves. Literature offers not only a new insight into 'reality' but also reveals the formal operations whereby what is commonly taken for 'reality' is constructed.

Ortega y Gasset's comments on the 'dehumanization of art' afford a fruitful comparison here. Arguing that our access to reality is always conceptually structured in some way, Ortega contends that our direct experience of persons, things, situations, the way in which we 'live' them, is granted a position of primacy in being taken for 'reality itself'. It is this concept which Ortega designates as human reality, arguing that the peculiarity of modern art consists in its tendency to 'dehuman-ize' reality by shattering the concept of reality as it is directly 'lived' and experienced. 'By divesting them of their aspect of "lived" reality,' he writes, 'the artist has blown up the bridges and burned the ships that could have taken us back to our daily world.'[11] However, art does not merely 'dehumanize' reality as it is lived by depriving it of its spontaneity and directness. It also offers an insight into the construc-tions of that lived reality itself, making them appear 'lean and angular', 'pure and transparent'.[12]

The Formalists proposed two main candidates with regard to the habitual modes of perception which literature was said to work on and transform. First, particularly with regard to poetry, literature was said to effect a semantic shift in relation to prosaic language by playing on and subverting the conventional relationship between signifier and signified, opening up the web of language into a play of multiple meanings excluded from ordinary speech.

Second, literary works were said to defamiliarize the codes and con-ventions of previous traditions which, although they had once them-selves served as a means of perceptual dislocation, have since atrophied to become the source of perceptual numbness. 'The fate of the works of bygone artists of the word', Shklovsky maintained, 'is the same as the fate of the word itself: both shed light on the path from poetry to prose; both become coated with the glass armour of the familiar.'[13] In this sense, literature is a play of form upon form. It uses one set of devices to chisel the ground from beneath another, usually canonical or revered set of devices and, in doing so, wrestles 'reality' away from the terms of seeing they propose, thereby making it the focus of a renewed interest and attentiveness. At the risk of simplification, literature might thus be construed as a mode of discourse which constantly main-tains 'No, the world is not like that' in relation to dominant forms of discourses which maintain that it is.

Literature, then, is a practice of transformation. It works on and transforms the raw materials provided by other literary works, ordin-ary language, and so on. It is important to note, however, that such raw materials do not exist solely in forms which are external to the text. The old and the new, the defamiliarized and the defamiliarizing coexist within the text as different levels. As Jakobson put it:

> It was the Formalist research which clearly demonstrated that shifting and change are not only historical statements (first there was A, then A₁ arose in place of A) but that shift is also a directly experienced synchronic phenomenon, a relevant artistic value. The reader of a poem or the viewer of a painting has a vivid awareness of two orders: the traditional canon and the artistic novelty as a deviation from that canon.[14]

This throws into relief the truly abstract and relational character of the category of literariness. For, given that the process of defamiliarization is essentially a play of form upon form, it is clear that a text which may be regarded as 'literary' in one historical situation may, in another, stand on the other side of the equation. Put another way, 'the dominant' of literature – defamiliarization – is a shifting dominant so that whether or in what respects a text is to be regarded as 'literary' depends on the point from which it is viewed.

There thus exists an element of indetermination as to what counts as 'literature' and what does not. Certainly, 'literature' is not regarded as an immutable body of texts but as a function variably fulfilled by different texts in different circumstances. In effect, the Formalists did not study texts at all but the apparently more abstract – although, in reality, more concrete – object of the system of relationships between texts.

AGAINST THE 'METAPHYSIC OF THE TEXT'

We must again refer to Saussure here. As we have seen, Saussure argued that the origin of a given unit of language could throw no light on its present-day use and meaning within the system of *la langue*. The Formalists, maintaining a similar position with regard to the origin of a literary device and its function within a given text, applied the same principle to the question of the value and function of literary texts themselves. A text's standing as 'literature' – its ability to fulfil the function of defamiliarization – was not given for all time but was said to depend on the nature of the relationships it established with other texts within a given 'literary system'.

Jurij Tynyanov thus argued that the classification of a text as 'literary' depended on its 'differential quality, that is, on its relationship with both literary and extra-literary orders'.[15] It is this concept of a particular set of relationships between the 'literary' and the 'extra-literary' orders that Tynyanov had in mind in his concept of 'literary system'. His contention was that the same text – he mentions the case of certain diaries – may take on a 'literary' or a 'non-literary' function according to the nature of the literary system within which it is set. Furthermore, he suggests that it is only by ignoring the different values and functions which the same text may assume in different moments of its history as a received text that more conventional schools of criticism construct the literary traditions to which they address themselves:

> Tradition, the basic concept of the established history of literature, has proved to be an unjustifiable abstraction of one or more of the literary elements of a given system within which they occupy the same plane and play the same role. They are equated with the like elements of another system in which they are on a different plane, thus they are brought into a seemingly unified, fictitiously integrated system.[16]

A similar notion of literature's relative status is involved in Shklovsky's 'law of the canonization of the junior branch'. According to this, the themes and motifs of such 'junior' or 'sub-literary' genres as the thriller or the romance are said to provide the devices whereby literature renews itself, moving beyond those forms which, although once defamiliarizing in relation to some previous norm of the familiar, have themselves since become ossified. Two cases may be distinguished.

The first concerns those instances in which particular literary forms renew themselves by drawing upon the themes and devices of 'junior' or 'sub-literary' genres. In such cases there is no question of the 'junior' genres concerned crossing the line between the 'sub-literary' and the 'literary'. It is merely that the same devices take on different functions when they are put to different uses in different contexts. The Formalists, for example, were very interested in the role which the use of certain stock-in-trade devices of the detective story had played in renovating the Russian novel, as in the involved use of 'whodunnit' conventions in Dostoevsky's *Brothers Karamazov*. Their point, however, was not that the detective stories on which Dostoevsky drew had thus become 'literature' but that 'literature' had been renewed, in Dostoevsky's works, by using devices from the detective novel to 'make strange', subvert and break away from the prevailing canons of novelistic realism.

The second case concerns the shift in the standing that may be accorded a particular text during different moments of its historical existence as a received text. As the history of criticism amply confirms, a text previously regarded as unexceptional may be retrospectively 'canonized' in coming to assume a literary function and value and, in some cases, fulfilling a renovative role within the literary field in general. In the same way a text, once granted a position of pivotal importance, may subsequently be relegated to the penumbral regions of literature. Shklovsky's point here is not the familiar one that literary texts may rise and fall in favour with changes in 'literary taste'. It is rather that the position of any single text in relation to other texts, and hence its function, is liable to constant shifts and displacements as new forms of writing transform and reorganize the entire system of relationships between texts.

In recognizing these migrations of marginal literary forms into the centre of literature and back again to the periphery, the Formalists tended to dissolve the concerns of aesthetics and to nudge them in the direction of history. Ultimately, the concept of 'literature' which they proposed referred not to a fixed body of texts whose literariness was guaranteed by their conformity to a universal and unchanging set of formal attributes, but to particular and changing sets of *relationships between texts*. The effect of this was to induce a 'binocular vision' of literary texts which enabled their value and function to be viewed differently according to the different places they occupied within the received cultures of different societies and different historical periods.

This is not, of course, to argue that the objective material and organizational properties of literary texts change from one period to another. It is rather to recognize that those properties do not themselves suffice to guarantee a text's literariness. In effect, literariness depends crucially not on the formal properties of a text in themselves but on the position which those properties establish for the text within the matrices of the prevailing ideological field. Literariness resides, not in the text, but in the relations of inter-textuality inscribed within and between texts. It is not a 'thing', an essence which the text possesses, but a function which the text fulfils. And whether or not a particular text fulfils this function depends, in part, on determinations which are situated outside and independently of that text.

A certain degree of arbitrariness might thus be said to be attached to the question of a text's literariness in much the same way as, for Saussure, the relationship between signifier and signified is arbitrary in the sense that there is no intrinsic connection between sound and meaning binding the two. This does not constitute a flight away from historical considerations so much as a mode of entry into them. 'Because it is arbitrary', Jonathan Culler has argued, 'the sign is totally subject to history, and the combination at a particular moment of a given signifier and signified is a contingent result of the historical process.'[17] In the same way, it is not the text's origins or its purely formal properties which determine its literariness but its mode of functioning within a society's culture as determined by its contingent, and therefore historical and changing relations with other cultural forms.

Why is this important? Mainly because it requires us to perceive 'literature' in a historical and concrete fashion and not abstractly. One must adopt a 'binocular vision' in relation to the text, studying it as a concrete, historically changing entity subject to different determinations in the different ways in which it is appropriated and the different sets of intertextual relationships in which it is placed during different moments of its history as a received text. To posit the concept of the text outside of such matrices or to speak of its 'effect' – aesthetic or political – independently of such considerations is to fall prey to a 'metaphysic of the text': to a conception of the text as an abstraction which transcends history.

The Formalists' critique of the 'metaphysic of the text' was, however, a purely abstract one. For the process whereby the value and function of a text might be subject to variation was never really analysed or explained by them but was rather presented as something which 'simply happened'. This reflects a deeper problem. For, although the Formalists were able to allow historical considerations (albeit in an abstract form) a central role in determining the value and function of literary texts, they were unable to integrate such considerations into their account of the process whereby particular forms and genres are themselves subject to change and development.

THE PROBLEM OF LITERARY EVOLUTION

The notorious weak spot of Saussure's theory of language lies, as we shall see later, in its inability to account for the processes and mechanisms whereby the system of rules comprising *la langue* are subject to change through time. The most that Saussure offered was a theory of mutations according to which innovations in usage are said to produce a situation of disequilibrium within the system of *la langue*. Change, by this account, results from the tendency of *la langue*, as a self-regulating system, to restore a state of equilibrium by effecting a series of counterbalancing mutations.

The Formalists' account of literary evolution suffered from similar weaknesses. Where the Formalists were strongest was in pointing to the relationships of 'exchange' within literature whereby, at a purely formal level, literary change could be seen to be produced. For Shklovsky, as we have seen, literature renewed itself partly by plundering the devices of marginal literary works. Elsewhere, both Shklovsky and Eichenbaum maintained that the renovation of literature was frequently effected by writers having recourse to the literary devices of earlier and often neglected literary traditions. It was this that they had in mind in their famous aphorism to the effect that the line of literary influence runs not from father to son but from grandfather to grandson or from uncle to nephew. However, although thus able to point to the sources from which innovatory writers derived their models, the Formalists conspicuously failed to explain either the particular direction of the path of literary development or its historical curvature. Instead, literary evolution was viewed as the result of a purely abstract dialectic of 'the negation of the negation' with new codes and devices being called into being as those which preceded them were said to have reached a point of exhaustion or to have degenerated into formal clichés.

Boris Eichenbaum's *The Young Tolstoy* illustrates these problems nicely. Arguing that Tolstoy was writing during a period when the canonical forms of the Russian romantic tradition were becoming 'accessible and easy', Eichenbaum views Tolstoy's works as embodying 'a process of making these canonized forms difficult again by breaking them down and mixing them, on the one hand, and by reviving old, long forgotten traditions, on the other'.[18] By reviewing Tolstoy's early works as well as the evidence of his diaries, Eichenbaum shows that Tolstoy virtually ignored the romantic tradition itself in favour of the grand philosophical writers of the late eighteenth and early nineteenth centuries (Goethe and Scott in particular) and such noted parodists of the novel as Sterne and Rousseau. He argues that Tolstoy used a stock of devices culled from these sources in order to effect a 'bestrangement' of the canons of Russian romanticism.

His account of the means whereby Tolstoy 'bestranges' the romantic idealization of war affords a useful illustration. He points out how, in both The Sevastopol Sketches and War and Peace, Tolstoy follows Stendhal's portrayal of the battle of Waterloo in The Charterhouse of Parma in effecting a 'bestrangement' of the romantic concept of battle via the device of the novice who, initially conceiving of war in accordance with the usual romantic stereotypes, is brutally disillusioned by his first contact with it. Perhaps Eichenbaum's most illuminating insight, however, is his analysis of the role of Tolstoy's narrative style, particularly in its close attention to detailed, almost naturalist description of minutiae, as itself a device of 'bestrangement' in relation to romantic stereotypes. As he writes of The Sevastopol Sketches:

> The battle scenes are bestranged by everyday details which not unparadoxically, are placed in the foreground: ' "That's *him* firing from the new battery today," adds the old man, *indifferently spitting* on his hand'. . . . A young officer complains that it is bad at the fourth bastion, not because of the bombs or bullets, as one might expect, but 'because it's muddy'. At the bastion itself . . . sailors play cards under the breastworks and an officer '*calmly rolls a cigarette out of yellow paper*'. The latter detail is reinforced by its repetition after a description of a wounded sailor: ' "Every day it's some seven or eight men that get it," the naval officer tells you, answering the expression of horror expressed on your face, *yawning and rolling a cigarette out of yellow paper*.' The officer gives the command to fire, and the sailors

'promptly, cheerfully, one *thrusting a pipe in his pocket, another finishing up a rusk*, clattering on the platform with their hobnailed boots, go off to the cannon and load it.'[19]

For Eichenbaum, then, Tolstoy's essential literary orientation is to say, in relation to the conventions of romanticism: 'No, things are not like that. People do not live, love and die as it is written. Nature is not as it is portrayed.' As such, his approach to Tolstoy is purely poetic: it describes the relation between the canons of romanticism and Tolstoy's 'bestrangement' of them as a relationship internal to Tolstoy's texts themselves. The only historical considerations that are brought into the picture concern the literary sources from which Tolstoy derived his devices of 'bestrangement'. No account is offered for the motivation behind Tolstoy's 'bestrangement' of romantic forms other than that of a purely artistic will to break with literary canons whose apparent ossification is attributed solely to the passage of time itself rather than to any change in the structure of social, political and ideological relationships. Nor is any attempt made to relate Tolstoy's literary ambitions to the social, political or ideological aspirations of any wider social forces.

Of course, at one level, this may simply have reflected Eichenbaum's decision to focus on certain matters at the expense of others. Yet the evidence suggests that, even when the Formalists explicitly acknowledged the need to take into account social and political factors in order to account for literary change, they proved incapable of proposing a method which would accomplish this. Nor is this surprising. For any progress in this direction required a revaluation of Saussure's legacy. Fredric Jameson argues:

> Once you have begun by separating diachronic from synchronic . . . you can never really put them back together again. If the opposition in the long run proves to be a false or misleading one, then the only way to suppress it is by throwing the entire discussion on to a higher dialectical plane, choosing a new starting point, utterly recasting the problems involved in new terms. . . .[20]

4

FORMALISM AND BEYOND

THE ACCOMPLISHMENTS OF FORMALISM

In his essay 'On Realism in Art', Jakobson summarized the Formalists' perception of the intellectual flabbiness of the traditional schools of literary criticism they sought to displace:

> Until recently, the history of art, particularly that of literature, has had more in common with causerie than with scholarship. It obeyed all the laws of causerie, skipping blithely from topic to topic, from lyrical effusions on the elegance of forms to anecdotes from the artist's life, from psychological truisms to questions concerning philosophical significance and social environment. . . . The history of art has been equally slipshod with respect to scholarly terminology. It has employed the current vocabulary without screening the words critically, without defining them precisely, and without considering the multiplicity of their meanings.[1]

Perhaps the most significant achievement of the Formalists consisted in their recognition that the word 'literature' would have to be 'screened critically' if it were to serve any useful purpose. In proposing a highly specific meaning for the term, the Formalists placed their literary criticism on a self-consciously theoretical footing by rigorously defining the object – the literariness of literary discourse – to which it should address itself.

Although the type of study that the Formalists thus proposed was still an aesthetic – a theory of 'literature' as such – it was essentially a scientific aesthetic. Breaking entirely with attempts to explain the particular quality of the literary text with reference to its origin in some capacity – usually 'the genius' – of the person who wrote it, the Formalists sought to resolve the question of literature's specificity empirically by considering the formal properties governing the structure of literary texts.

In doing so, the Formalists also called into question the concerns of reflection theory. In showing that all literary forms were equally and necessarily a semiotic mediation of reality, a *signification* of reality and not a *reflection* of it, they cast doubt on the validity or usefulness of any debate about the degree of verisimilitude attained by literary texts. The term 'realism', they argued, could only be of value if, shorn of its literalness, it were used to refer to those conventionalized systems of literary representation – notably the nineteenth-century novel – which generate the illusion that they are transcriptions of reality, forms in which the real appears to 'write itself'.

Finally, although their own work reflected the concerns of traditional aesthetics, they simultaneously undermined those concerns by suggesting that the literariness of a text depends not solely on its intrinsic properties but on its value and function, on the relationship it establishes with other texts in different 'literary systems'. 'Since a system is not an equal interaction of all elements,' Tynyanov wrote, 'but places a group of elements in the foreground – the "dominant" – and thus involves the deformation of the remaining elements, a work enters into literature and takes on its own literary function through this dominant.'[2] But 'the dominant' through which a text enters into literature – its ability to defamiliarize – is essentially a relational property. A text can fulfil the literary function of defamiliarization only in relation to some established norm of the familiar. But as this, too, is liable to change, then the function of any given text must itself vary as between different moments of its historical existence.

It is thus only from the point of view of historical scholarship that the realist conventions of the nineteenth-century novel can be regarded as having, in the Formalist sense, a 'literary function'. From the stand-point of contemporary cultural practice, they stand on the other side of the equation: they represent the 'familiar' against which much contemporary literature turns its face.

This perception of the changing value and function of literary texts involved challenging the notion that the organization into which the texts constituting a given literary tradition are compressed is in any sense an organization of, in Leavis's phrase, 'similarly placed things'. To the contrary, it is the practice of criticism which itself does the placing and, as Tynyanov noted, often by positing as part of the same tradition texts which occupy different positions and fulfil different functions in different literary systems.

Our own received literary tradition, for example, is customarily presented as an uninterrupted line of development running from the Greeks through a smattering of late medieval writers and the Renaissance humanists on to the mainstream of bourgeois poetry, drama and the novel to which there is added, although more tenta-tively, a selection of 'modern classics'. Yet it is clear that this is a highly selective and, in some senses, arbitrary orchestration of past and pres-ent cultural practice, the result of a set of operations upon the texts concerned rather than the reflection of any necessary or intrinsic connection between them.

The point is well illustrated in the response of Étienne Balibar and Pierre Macherey to Marx's question: 'Where does the eternal charm of Greek art come from?':[3]

There is no good answer to this question, quite simply because there is no eternal charm in Greek art: for the *Iliad*, a fragment of universal literature, used in this instance as a vehicle for memory, is not the *Iliad* produced by the material life of the Greeks, which was not a 'book' nor even a 'myth' in our sense of the word, which we would like to apply retrospectively. Homer's *Iliad*, the 'work' of an 'author' exists only for us, and in relation to new material conditions into which it has been reinscribed and reinvested with a new significance: however odd it may seem, it did not exist for the Greeks and the problem of its conservation is thus not a relevant one. To go further: it is as if we ourselves had written it (or at least composed it anew). Works of art are processes and not objects, for they are never produced once and for all, but are continually susceptible to 'reproduction': in fact, they only find an identity and a content in this continual process of transformation. There is no eternal art, there are no fixed and immutable works.[4]

A given literary tradition, then, is not simply an inheritance, a reflection of things that are and always have been 'similarly placed', but is an active construction, a particular form of the cultural appropriation of representations 'handed down' from the past.[5] This naturally calls into question the concerns of traditional aesthetics. For it is only a particular, historically produced reconstruction of the texts concerned which suggests that there should be any fundamental commonalty between Homer and Balzac, Aeschylus and Shakespeare, which is to be investigated as part of a theory of the specificity of 'literature', as part of an aesthetic.

The Formalists, in complex and contradictory ways, administered the funeral rites to aesthetics in this sense. As we have seen, they theorized not 'works' – not a fixed and immutable set of texts – but changing functions and relationships between texts. In doing so, they undermined the 'metaphysic of the text' which underlies the bulk of both conventional and Marxist criticism: namely, the assumption that the text has a once-and-for-all existence, a once-and-for-all relationship to other texts which is marked and determined by the circumstances of its origin. The Formalists, by contrast, studied the text as a historically changing entity, giving rise to different 'effects' in the light of the different determinations to which it is subjected during its history.

It has already been pointed out that their understanding of these processes was, however, purely abstract. Although they argued that the system of relationships between texts which determined the value and function of any given text was subject to a perpetual, kaleidoscopic oscillation, they could offer no account of the mechanisms whereby this oscillation was produced.

At root, this reflected their inability to deal with the problem of literary change. For both shortcomings rested on the same fundamental flaw: the inability to relate internal mechanisms of change within literature to external forces of propulsion. Although the Formalists tried to link these two dimensions, they were, as was suggested above, prevented from doing so by the theoretical heritage they derived from Saussure.

SAUSSURE'S MAGIC CARPET

It would be difficult to overestimate the influence of Saussure on twentieth-century thought. Quite apart from his impact on linguistics, we have seen that his work has formed the basis for the structuralist projection 'that all social practices can be understood as meanings, as significations and as circuits of exchange between subjects, and can therefore lean on linguistics as a model for the elaboration of their systematic reality'.[6] Whilst there is little doubt that this projection has made much work possible that would otherwise have been unimaginable, particularly in the evidence it has afforded of the systemic properties of cultural forms as diverse as folk tales and fashion, certain real difficulties have recently become evident:

(i) *Reductionism.* Ultimately, as Jakobson's later work on poetry suggests, the analogy with language entails the denial of the specificity of such cultural forms as poetry and literature as it implies that their study is to be pushed back into and made dependent on the study of language.

(ii) *Formalism.* 'The structure', Terence Hawkes writes, with Saussure's concept of *la langue* in mind, 'is not static. The laws which govern it act so as to make it not only structured, but *structuring*. Thus, in order to avoid reduction to the level merely of passive form, the structure must be capable of *transformational* procedures, whereby new material is constantly processed by and through it.'[7] True: but this is to *reify* the structure, to make it the subject of its own process. Instead of being viewed as a concept, the structure is viewed as a thing – a real entity – with a life and will of its own. Saussure's concept of *la langue*, for example, initially conceived as merely a systematization of the rules which make individual speech-acts possible, was subsequently granted all the attributes of a person or philosophical subject in being endowed with the capability to undertake operations in relation to itself. This is clearly exemplified in Saussure's conception of the process whereby *la langue* undertakes a series of internal adjustments in order to accommodate and cancel out the disturbing effects of those mutations of usage which fail to comply with its rules.

(iii) *Idealism.* Tzvetan Todorov has argued that the real concern of structuralism, as applied to literature, is with 'the system of literary discourse in so far as this is the generative principle behind any and every text'.[8] In his *A Theory of Literary Production*, Pierre Macherey objects that to explain a literary text in this way is to deny its real complexity by reducing it to the level of a mere resemblance of the structure which is thus said to be contained within it. The result is a form of Platonic idealism in which the real text is represented as a mere shadow cast by an ideal essence, a variant manifestation of some essential structure which is said to be visible through it. Criticism, on this construction, is a process of 'reading through' the text to reveal the purely ideal and disembodied structure which is said to underlie and produce it.

(iv) *Anthropologism.* Structuralism rests on an anthropological conception of 'man the communicator' with the result that the study of culture is entered exclusively through the problematic of the exchange of messages. Thus it entirely omits any consideration of the processes whereby new cultural forms are brought into being. The most that can be offered is an abstract typology of cultural forms which lack any anchorage in the social and historical circumstances of their production.

These criticisms, of course, relate not merely to structuralism but to the Saussurian premises which underlie it. Saussure's separation of the synchronic study of *la langue* as a system of rules frozen at a given point in time from the diachronic study of the forces regulating the historical development of language is particularly important in this respect. This is not to say that there is anything wrong with this distinction. Viewed abstractly, it is of considerable methodological value and, in intention at least, Saussure proposed the distinction purely for the methodological yield to be gained from it. He was primarily concerned with the system of conventions which make possible the production and exchange of messages between members of the same language community. That the social and historical processes whereby such conventions are produced, sustained or changed might also be a worthwhile object of study Saussure did not, of course, deny. He merely contended that such considerations of diachrony would not greatly further our understanding of the mechanisms by which meaning is produced within a given system of language rules.

The difficulty is that Saussure so construed and handled the distinction between the synchronic and diachronic levels of analysis as to suggest not merely a contrast between different *methodological perspectives* on language but also a whole series of related distinctions concerning the *substantive nature* of language itself. The synchronic/diachronic distinction thus parallels the distinction between *la langue* and *la parole*, between what is taken to be the truly social side of language, comprised by the rules of *la langue*, and its more contingent or individual aspects comprised by the particular uses to which those rules are put by different speakers within the events of *la parole*. In effect, by driving a methodological wedge between the synchronic and the diachronic, Saussure also drove a substantive wedge between those facets of language which, in their dialectical interplay, can alone explain the tempo and direction of language change.

These difficulties are exacerbated by the fact that, for Saussure, language is social in a purely abstract sense. For, as a body of rules pre-existing the individual, *la langue* is conceived of as a totally unitary system. The storehouse and embodiment of an undifferentiated societal collective consciousness, it gives rise merely to the concept of the ideal-typical speaker and has no room for the concept of different, class-based linguistic practices: that is, of *different communities of speakers who bring different sets of rules into play in their uses of language*. Small wonder that change could not be accounted for. For the very motor of change – conflict and difference – had been exiled from the heartland of language.

The methodological artifice of the distinction between the synchronic and the diachronic levels of analysis thus had its price. Whilst it enabled Saussure to address the problem of the systemic nature of language, it provided no means by which the problem of change could be addressed. Saussure was, as a result, forced either to sidestep this problem or to seek to resolve it at the price of an extreme reification. 'Time,' he wrote, in an almost hopeless gesture, 'changes all things; there is no reason why language should escape this universal law.'[9]

Time, the index of change, is thus converted into its explanation; change is merely the effect of the time which measures it.

Alternatively, change is explained as the product of the *sui generis* transformations which *la langue* undertakes in order to cancel out the disequilibrium induced by those changes in usage which break its strictures. This, as we have noted, has the effect of transforming *la langue* from a concept into a reified 'real' entity, a subject which oversees and regulates its own processes. More fundamentally, perhaps, no explanation is offered as to how it is possible that such 'disturbing' patterns of usage should arise in face of the edicts of *la langue* in the first place. These, as it were, 'just happen'. Chance and necessity thus play a gleeful game of tag with one another in Saussure's theory of language change as first the one and then the other is allowed a central role. First, necessity rules as all utterances are produced in compliance with the rules of *la langue*; then chance has its say as these rules are accidently and unaccountably broken; finally necessity reasserts itself as the iron laws of *la langue* take over to counterbalance the effects of such accidental deviations.

This inability to deal with the problem of change, of course, had a further consequence: namely, that the system of rules comprising *la langue* at any point in time is never itself explained but is merely described and systematized. Language hobbles on from one synchronic system of *la langue* to another without any adequate account being offered as to how it does so or as to why, at a particular point in time, the particular system of rules which comprise *la langue* take the form that they do.

The legacy the Formalists derived from Saussure was thus essentially a double-edged one. On the one hand, in taking over the Saussurian distinction between function and origin, the Formalists were able to place at the centre of their inquiries the concept of the variable functions fulfilled by particular texts as determined by the different and changing 'literary systems' in which they were set. They approached a given text in the same way that Saussure approached a unit of language. Just as the function and meaning of the latter is determined not by its origin but by its relationship to other such units of meaning within the system of relationships comprised by *la langue*, so the function and meaning of a text derives from its relationship to other texts within a given 'literary system'.

In this sense, the concepts of 'literary system' and la langue might be regarded as parallel concepts. Both refer to systems of relationships which organize and determine the function and meaning of the elements (literary texts and units of language respectively) which comprise them. As such, however, they suffer from similar defects. Just as no account is offered of the means whereby la langue moves from one synchronic state to another, so, although we know that 'literary systems' – and the functioning of particular texts within these – change, the Formalists could not explain how or why these changes take place. In a sense, Saussure's concept of la langue and the Formalists' concept of 'literary system' are a little like oriental flying carpets: both hover in the air, taking off in this direction or that and, as no explanation is offered of the means by which they are thus propelled, one can only conclude that they are magical.

BAKHTIN'S HISTORICAL POETICS

We can see, then, both the radical potential of the Formalists' work and, at the same time, the limitations which curtailed that potential. Whilst they dissolved the concerns of aesthetics into those of history, they did so only abstractly and, having produced questions that were inescapably historical, had no means of resolving them.

The project of a historical poetics proposed by Mikhail Bakhtin and Pavel Medvedev in the late 1920s was an attempt to realize this potential. Working through the Formalists, they set out to go beyond them, to chart a terrain for Marxist criticism that would be unremittingly historical. There takes place in their works a dialogue between the concerns of Formalism and those of Marxism which, although it was, as Seldon puts it, 'unconcluded', was nevertheless extraordinarily productive.

However, we must first consider some aspects of Valentin Vološinov's Marxism and the Philosophy of Language.[10] First published in 1929, this work ranks as the first systematic attempt to develop a Marxist theory of language which reflected a thorough grounding in linguistics. In subjecting the categories of Saussurian linguistics to critical analysis, Vološinov produced a new, historical approach to the study of language which provides the necessary theoretical back-cloth against which the work of Bakhtin and Medvedev must be viewed.

It was to Saussure's designation of *la langue* as the proper object of linguistics that Vološinov took most violent exception. This was chiefly because, in Vološinov's estimation, it did violence to the position of the speaker who, he argued, orientates to language not as a system of invariant rules with which he must comply but as a field of possibilities which he is to utilize in concrete utterances in particular social contexts. The proper object of linguistics for Vološinov, then, was not the fixed system of *la langue* but the ways in which the rules comprising it are used, modified and adapted in concrete utterances, the determinations of which are exclusively social. A concern with the linguistic sign as the product of particular and differing sociolinguistic relationships was thus substituted for Saussure's concern with 'the relationship of sign to sign within a closed system'.[11]

In order to effect such a theoretical shift, Vološinov argued that it was necessary to abandon Saussure's contention that meaning is produced solely by virtue of the relationships of similarity and difference which exist between signs within the closed system of *la langue*. One must also, he argued, take account of the fact that, in concrete utterances, the structure, meaning and use of the linguistic sign – the word – is inherently 'dialogical'. The word, that is, is orientated to and takes account of the use of words in the utterances to which it is a response or in the utterances which it seeks to solicit as a response. Vološinov contended that these dialogic relationships must be placed at the centre of analysis if the mechanisms whereby meaning is produced within language were to be properly understood.

This position was, in part, derived from Vološinov's reflections on the Formalists' concern with the problem of *skaz* – that is, of the position which the speaking subject adopts in relation to the language s/he uses. However, it received its most adequate and fully worked out expression in Bakhtin's study of Dostoevsky.

Analysing the conventions according to which discourse is constructed in Dostoevsky's works, Bakhtin argues that the Dostoevskian word is inherently a 'side-glancing word'. Dostoevsky's characters, that is, never speak without immediately altering or qualifying their discourse in the light of the possible reactions of some real (another character) or imaginary (the reader) interlocutor. The word is thus, within such a discourse, constantly looking over its shoulder and, ever-sensitive to the words of others, is subject to incessant modification. Used in this way, the word reflects and effects a particular set of relationships between speaker and listener within language itself and can only be fully understood when its functioning within the context of such relationships is properly appreciated.

Vološinov's first proposed modification of Saussurian linguistics, then, was to suggest that the word should be understood not only along the axes of its relationship to other words but in the context of its functioning within the dialogic relationships between speaker and listener. These, to avoid confusion, referred not to the objective social relationships between a real flesh-and-blood speaker and an equally material listener but to the relationships between the *role* of speaker and the *role* of listener as constructed by and within particular language forms or discourses. His second, and perhaps more radical step was to argue that such language forms or, as he called them, 'speech-genres' might themselves be explained with reference to the objective 'conditions of socio-verbal interaction' on which they are predicated.

It is arguable that the root source of Saussure's difficulties consisted in his separation of the system of rules internal to *la langue* from any practices located outside that system. Ultimately, it is Saussure's concept of the arbitrary relation between signifier and signified that is crucially debilitating here. In itself, of course, the concept is unexceptionable. Indeed, it is essential to an understanding of the historicity of language in the respect that, by denying any intrinsic connection binding signifier and signified, form and meaning, it presents that relation as being subject to historical variation and determination. But, within Saussure's work, it is only the variation and never the determination that is explained.

Raymond Williams has suggested that the explanation for this is attributable to the (incorrect) assumption that, because the relationship between signifier and signified is arbitrary in the sense of being conventional, it must also be arbitrary in the sense that it displays no necessary or demonstrable relation to the historical processes by which, as a particular unit of meaning, it is produced. 'On the contrary,' he argues, 'the fusion of formal element and meaning . . . is the result of a real process of social development, in the actual activities of speech and in the continuing development of a language.'[12]

The call here is for a theory of language which will explain the particular unity of form and meaning established by the system of signs which constitute language with reference to the socially based and historically changing linguistic practices on which that system rests. It was to precisely just such a theory that Vološinov addressed himself. His concern was not with language in isolation, however, but as part of an attempt to develop a comprehensive theory of ideology within Marxism.

As the concept of ideology has had a varied and chequered career within the history of Marxism, we must be clear about the way in which Vološinov used it. Briefly, in speaking of 'ideology', he had in mind the totality of those conventionalized forms through which sense and meaning are conferred on 'reality'. The plane of ideology is thus equated with that of semiotics – the world of signs – and, as such, is objective and material in nature. Ideology, Vološinov argues, is not the abstract product of an equally abstract 'consciousness' but has an autonomous and objective existence as either a distinctive, culturally encoded organization of sound waves (speech, music) or a codified co-ordination of light rays (print, visual images) effected by the manipulation of material substances. Unlike other planes of reality, however, the plane of ideology also 'reflects and refracts', in accordance with its own principles of organization, a reality outside itself. The sign, in other words, not only exists: it *signifies*.

It is the double-edged nature of this concept of the sign that is vital. For Saussure, all that matters is the relationship of one sign to another within the closed system of *la langue*; the question of their referent outside language is entirely 'bracketed'. This means, as we have seen, that there is no way in which the structure of *la langue* can be explained with reference to determinations which lie outside it. For Vološinov, by contrast, although language and, in a more general sense, all ideological forms are granted an autonomous reality of their own, imposing a signification on 'reality' which reflects their own systemic organization, these forms, although not reducible to economic and social relationships are, in part, explicable by them. For it is not the abstract grammar of language that interests Vološinov but rather the uses to which the rules comprising this grammar are put in concrete social situations. His primary concern was to establish a typology of speech forms or genres and to explain these with reference to the conditions of socioverbal interaction on which they rest and by which they are produced.

The sign, in its actual and concrete usage, is thus always socially formed. Its actual use and meaning, in the case of language, is reciprocally determined by *whose* word it is and *for whom* it is meant. It is always set within and, in part, moulded by a particular set of social relationships between speaker and listener: that is, by particular conditions of socioverbal interaction which are themselves moulded by the broader social, economic and political relationships in which they are set. Given that all language forms are predicated on distinctive, historically produced relationships between speaker(s) and listener(s) – Vološinov mentions such cases as drawing-room conversation and language etiquette – the central analytical task is to determine how those language forms are determined by the relationships on which they are articulated and to specify how, in their inner organization, they 'refract' or signify those relationships:

> This is the order that the actual generative process of language follows: social intercourse is generated (stemming from the basis); in it, verbal communication and interaction are generated; and in the latter, forms of speech performance are generated; finally, this generative process is reflected in the change of language forms.[13]

Thus there is, in Vološinov's work, a constant toing and froing between language forms and the social relationships in which they are set – between, in short, sign and reality. However, this is not to say that language is subject to change and development simply in response to the changes which take place in the conditions of socioverbal intercourse. Change also results from the elements of contradiction and instability located within language itself.

In systematizing the rules comprising *la langue*, Vološinov argued, Saussure tended to smooth out the discrepancies of meaning which may be attached to the same words by virtue of the different uses to which they are put in different, socially produced linguistic practices. It was by failing to recognize and deal with the theoretical consequences of the polysemanticity of the word – the word as the crossing-point of multiple meanings – that Saussure exiled the mechanisms of change from the heartland of language. Vološinov, by contrast, views the use of the word as part of a primarily class-based struggle for the terms in which reality is to be signified. Language, far from being a neutral horizon of fixed and given meanings, becomes an 'arena of class struggle' as words are mobilized and fought for by different class-based philosophies. It is by virtue of the interaction of 'differently oriented social interests within one and the same sign-community, i.e. by the class struggle',[14] that, Vološinov argues, language change can be accounted for as the result of mechanisms of contradiction inscribed within its very structure.

In summary, then, Vološinov argues that the proper concern of linguistics should be to establish a typology of speech genres which would explain the peculiar mode of the refraction or signification of reality they effect with reference to the social conditions of socio-verbal interaction, themselves contextualized within the framework of wider economic, social and political relationships, which underlie and produce them. This, for Vološinov, applied just as much to language in its written as in its spoken forms, just as much to literary genres – which he defined as 'verbal performances in print'[15] – as to speech genres.

It was in this respect that his work served as a backcloth to Medvedev's and Bakhtin's attempt to construct a sociologically and historically informed typology of literary genres. Vološinov provided the necessary concepts whereby the process of literary change could be analysed as a result of shifting class relationships. He also provided the means whereby the specificity of different forms of writing could be explained by referring them to the social relationships on which they are predicated.

It is the latter of these concerns which interests us here, particularly with regard to the way in which Bakhtin and Medvedev reworked the problem of literariness. By broaching the question of the specific nature of literature not as a separate issue but as merely one concern within a general theory of forms of writing, they provided that concern with a wider theoretical location and, in so doing, transformed it. The concern was no longer with 'literature' *per se* but with whether so-called 'literary' works 'have an autonomous ideological role and a type of refraction of socioeconomic existence entirely their own',[16] and, if so, how this might be explained in materialist terms.

They sought, in other words, to found a category of 'literature' that would be historically informed. The peculiar signification of 'reality' that literary works effected was to be explained not in idealist terms as the manifestation of some unchanging set of formal properties but as the product of a particular, socially constrained practice of writing and as the manifestation of a particular constellation of class relationships within language.

'LITERATURE' AS A HISTORICAL CATEGORY

We have already glanced at Bakhtin's work on Dostoevsky. His broader study of the 'carnivalization' of literature will serve to exemplify the issues involved here. What is 'carnivalized literature'? Bakhtin defines it as 'those genres which have come under the influence – either directly or indirectly, through a series of intermediary links – of one or another variant of carnivalistic folk-lore (ancient or medieval).'[17]

Although concerned with this phenomenon as a general problem in the history of poetics,[18] Bakhtin was more particularly interested in the 'carnivalization' of the major literary genres in the Renaissance as marking the birth of contemporary European *belles lettres*. For Renaissance literature, the world of carnival afforded a stock of themes and devices which permitted what Bakhtin calls the 'renewal' of medieval ideology: that is, the subversion of the fixed hierarchies it represented or, in other words, its defamiliarization.

The issues involved here are admirably illustrated in his *Rabelais and His World* (written in 1940, but not published until 1965). Ostensibly a study of the role of folk humour in Rabelais' work, it is also an attempt to account for the historical formation of contemporary European *belles lettres* as a new and distinctive form of writing predicated on a new set of social, political and ideological relationships.

In the classical medieval period, Bakhtin contends that the world of official medieval ideology and that of folk humour constituted two separate ideological spheres, totally opposed to one another, without any mediations or transition between them. The world of official medieval ideology, embodied in sacred texts and religious rituals and festivals, was one of an unrelieved, gloomy eschatology dominated by a view of existence in which God (and thence religious and secular authorities who held their power on lease from God) figured as the centre and pivot of the world. Completely opposed to this world and, in a sense, its mirror-image was the world of folk humour as embodied in popular rituals and festivals, especially carnivals, the comic shows of the marketplace and what Bakhtin calls the 'Billingsgate genres' – the popular oaths and curses of marketplace speech. Taken as a totality, these 'carnival' forms constituted a 'world turned upside down' in which the official, hierarchic representation of the world was inverted and, in some cases, 'decentred' – as in the popular feast which 'decentred' Christian ideology by placing the ass and not Jesus or Mary at its centre.

The world of folk humour thus constituted a *world apart* from official ideology and was a ritualized 'discrowning' of that ideology. 'They offered', Bakhtin wrote of these popular forms, 'a completely different, nonofficial, extraecclesiastical and extrapolitical aspect of the world and a second life outside officialdom, a world in which all medieval people participated more or less, in which they lived during a given time of the year.'[19] What was made available then, was not so much a 'renewal' or 'making strange' of ideology as an alternative, 'carnival' view of the world: a reversal of official ideology which was granted – largely because the people refused to relinquish it – a ritualized, semi-legal existence within the interstices of the Christian calendar.

The historical significance of such texts as Rabelais' *Gargantua and Pantagruel*, Bakhtin argues, was that they transformed the function of folk humour. No longer an accepted area of licence and reversal outside of and apart from official ideology, folk humour was, in the literature of the early Renaissance, brought into relation with the official ideology as part of a set of formal devices whereby that ideology was not merely parodied and inverted but transfixed and revealed, distanced *from within*, as the ideology of a crumbling world order:

> The culture of folk-humour that had been shaped during many centuries and that had defended the people's creativity in non-official forms, in verbal expression or spectacle, could now rise to the high level of literature and ideology and fertilize it. . . . This thousand year

old laughter not only fertilized literature but was itself fertilized by
humanist knowledge and advanced literary techniques.[20]

The meaning of this is perhaps most clearly illustrated by the principle of 'grotesque realism' which governed the world of folk humour
and by the uses to which Rabelais put this principle. According to this,
bodily imagery serves as a means of inverting the official social, moral
and political order. It is a system which has at its 'head' the anus and at
its 'heart' the belly. It is an image of the body as a devoured and
devouring totality which, related to the world through its orifices,
remains forever in a state of incompleteness.

Within its original popular setting, Bakhtin argues, the principle of
'grotesque realism' served both to invert established hierarchies and to
furnish a 'base' alternative to the officially sanctioned Christian eschatology. To the promise of heaven, it opposed an anatomical representation of a people's utopia: a world of surfeit and – there is no other
word for it – of gargantuan indulgence in the joys of the flesh.

With Rabelais, the function of 'grotesque realism' is transformed in
two ways. First, by constantly recasting the objects invested with ideological significance in the world of official culture – as when the belfry of
a monastery is likened to a phallus or a sermon to a prolonged fart –
Rabelais effects a 'degrading' and 'renewal' of objects, presenting them
in a new light by placing them in an unexpected context. In this way, the
entire world of medieval ideology is 'discrowned': that is, 'renewed' or
'made strange'. Second, bodily imagery is also used as a means of proposing another ideology in place of the official one. It is thus, Bakhtin
argues, that the concept of the body as a boundless, ever-onrolling entity,
swelling and expanding with each generation, served as a device for
expressing the newly emerging historical humanism of the Renaissance.

In a double movement, then, the principle of 'grotesque realism'
served both to define and limit medieval ideology and, by replacing the
concept of the ascent of the soul into heaven with that of the development of mankind, symbolized by bodily imagery, along the historical
axis of time, to substitute for it the formative historicist ideology of the
early Renaissance.

A couple of examples will, perhaps, help to make the point more
vividly. Bakhtin's analysis of the nature and function of Rabelais'

treatment of bells will serve to illustrate the formal means by which themes and devices derived from the world of carnival are used to subvert and belittle the official ideology of medieval Christian thought. Within the culture of the Middle Ages, bells took on two quite different functions and symbolic values according to the context in which they were used. Within the context of the official religious ideology, they functioned so as to symbolize spiritual values. Located in the belfries of churches and monasteries, they belonged to the world of 'the above'. Poised mid-way between the earth and heaven, the peals they tolled were a summons to men's higher calling. Within the world of carnival, however, in which cowbells were frequently tied to horses' halters and smaller bells were used as an accompaniment to festive feasting and dancing, bells were 'brought down' from their elevated position to take part in the world of 'the below', a world of festive merriment and excess. By wrenching church bells from the first of these contexts and placing them in the context of carnival, Bakhtin argues that Rabelais effects a limiting of official ideology, trampling its sombre seriousness underfoot beneath the merry dance of carnival.

It is thus that Gargantua, having relieved himself on the citizens of Paris from on top of the bell towers of Notre-Dame – itself, of course, a profound debasement of official ideology in its association of the most spiritual bells in the land with the lowest of bodily functions – decides to send the bells home to his father:

> After this exploit Gargantua examined the great bells that hung in those towers, and played a harmonious peal on them. As he did so it struck him that they would serve very well for cow-bells to hang on the collar of his mare, which he had decided to send to his father, loaded with Brie cheese and fresh herrings. So he took them straight off to his lodgings.[21]

We can see here how the great bells of Notre-Dame are 'brought down', in a movement of profound debasement, from their official exalted position to function in a carnival context – as cowbells – in association with the richest and most fulsome of festive food: Brie cheese and fresh herrings. Nothing could be less spiritual.

Our second example concerns the use of bodily imagery to symbolize the concept of the people as an ever-expanding, self-generating and regenerating historical force. It concerns the way in which Gargantua's mother, Gargamelle, was brought to bed by eating an excess of tripe:

> This was the manner in which Gargamelle was brought to bed – and if you don't believe it, may your fundament fall out! Her fundament fell out one afternoon, on the third of February, after she had over-eaten herself on *godebillios*. *Godebillios* are the fat tripes of *coiros*. *Coiros* are oxen fattened at the stall and in *guimo* meadows, and *guimo* meadows are those that carry two grass crops a year. They had killed three hundred and sixty-seven thousand and fourteen of these fat oxen to be salted down on Shrove Tuesday, so that in the spring they should have plenty of beef in season, with which to make a short *commemoration* at the beginning of meals, for the better enjoyment of their wine. The tripes were plentiful, as you will understand, and so appetizing that everyone licked his fingers. But the devil and all of it was that they could not possibly be kept any longer. For they were tainted, which seemed most improper. So it was resolved that they should be consumed without more ado . . .
>
> Now, the good man Grandgousier took very great pleasure in this feast and ordered that all should be served full ladles. Nevertheless he told his wife to eat modestly, seeing that her time was near and that this tripe was not very commendable meat. 'Anyone who eats the bag,' he said, 'might just as well be chewing dung.' Despite his warning, however, she ate sixteen quarters, two bushels, and six pecks. Oh, what fine faecal matter to swell up inside her![22]

And later, when Gargamelle's labour pains are indistinguishable from her bowel movements:

> A little while later she began to groan and wail and shout. Then suddenly swarms of midwives came up from every side, and feeling her underneath found some rather ill-smelling excrescences, which they thought were the child; but it was her fundament slipping out, because of the softening of her right intestine – which you call the bum-gut – owing to her having eaten too much tripe, as has been stated above.

At this point a dirty old hag of the company, who had the reputation of being a good she-doctor and had come from Brizepaille, near Saint Genou, sixty years before, made her an astringent, so horrible that all her sphincter muscles were stopped and constricted . . .

By this misfortune the cotyledons of the matrix were loosened at the top, and the child leapt up through them to enter the hollow vein. Then, climbing through the diaphragm to a point above the shoulders where this vein divides in two, he took the left fork and came out by the left ear.

As soon as he was born he cried out, not like other children: 'Mies! Mies!' but 'Drink! Drink! Drink!', as if inviting the whole world to drink, and so loud that he was heard through all the lands of Booze and Bibulous.[23]

There are many distinctively Rabelaisian elements at work in these passages: the material excess of festival feasting, for example, and the quite obviously 'debased' version of a miraculous birth which parodies, in its excess of scatological detail, the highly spiritual affair of divine conception. Bakhtin's concern, however, is more particularly with the functioning of tripe, bowels, faecal matter and foetus and with the eradication of the differences between them. It is an excess of tripe, the intestines of an animal, that induces in Gargamelle a bowel movement of such extraordinary power and duration that it is indistinguishable from her labour pains. Animal intestines, human intestines, faecal matter, foetus: all of these become one, part of a 'great belly' in which all events – eating, defecation, copulation, childbirth – take place and merge imperceptibly with one another. The resulting image is one of a single supraindividual bodily life, of the great bowels of mother earth which, in forever devouring and being devoured, symbolize the ever ongoing and regenerating body of the people, a merry, abundant, unstoppable force which 'opposes the serious medieval world of fear and oppression with all its intimidating and intimidated ideology'.[24]

To conclude, then, Bakhtin argues that Rabelais uses a set of devices culled from the world of folk humour to so 'work on' the categories of the dominant ideology of medieval society as to make them appear strange, to recast them within the world of carnival so that, instead of being filled with sombre seriousness, they are filled with belly laughter.

The important point, however, is that this effect of the 'renewal' of ideology is not regarded as something which typifies 'literature' as such. Offering his study as a pointer to the analysis of early Renaissance literature in general, Bakhtin views Rabelais' work as exemplifying a new form of writing – without parallel in medieval literature. Occupying a point mid-way between the folk-humour of popular culture and official medieval ideology, this new form of writing is the product of a new, historically produced set of social and cultural relationships which established some degree of connection between two cultural spheres which had hitherto been kept hermetically separate from one another:

> The Renaissance is the only period in the history of European literature which marked the end of a dual language and a linguistic transformation. Much of what was possible at that exceptional time later became impossible. It can be said of *belles lettres*, and especially of the modern novel, that they were born on the boundary of two languages. . . . An intense interorientation, interaction, and mutual clarification of languages took place during that period. The two languages frankly and intensely peered into each other's faces, and each became more aware of itself, of its potentialities and limitations, in the light of the other.[25]

Here, then, we have an approach to literature – meaning, here, all forms of fictional writing – that is historically and not aesthetically informed. Contemporary European *belles lettres* are distinguished from other forms of the practice of writing not as an instance of 'literature' as such, conceived of as an a-historical category, but in terms of the historical forces which bear on their production. The effect of 'renewal' in Rabelais' work is not simply given, as is the attribute of defamiliarization in Formalist writing, but derives from its position at the crossroads of two previously separate cultural systems. It exemplifies a new type of writing whose formal contours are determined precisely by the point of confluence at which it is situated – a confluence which, if culturally defined, has concrete social, political and ideological determinants.

Although these latter do not occupy the centre of Bakhtin's study, they are clearly implicated. The new form of writing which is the object of his study is granted a firm material base. Thus, if the classical medieval age offered no ideological space within which a literature of 'renewal' might be located, whereas the early Renaissance did, this reflected a number of developments. The undermining of Papal hegemony induced by the development of paper and print technology and by the spread of lay centres of education; the resulting interaction between popular culture and Church ideology effected by the new centrality granted to the vernacular; and the ideological and political crisis within feudalism created by the upsurge of dynastic nationalism and the development of a counter-hegemonic force in the urban burgher classes are among those that might be mentioned.[26] In short, the new form of writing introduced with the Renaissance is seen to have clear historical co-ordinates and determinants, the dismantling of official medieval ideology which it effected being viewed as part of the economic and political break-up of the feudal order.

Finally, to appreciate the full flavour of Bakhtin's historical method, it must be stressed that he in no sense attempts to reify Rabelais' work by imputing to it a 'once-and-for-all' function or effect abstracted from the real history of its existence as a received text. Apart from being a study of Rabelais, his work also offers a survey of Rabelais criticism. This makes it clear how, with the change in the political climate resulting from the onset of bourgeois and/or monarchical stability in the seventeenth and eighteenth centuries, an appreciation of the role and significance of the folk humour elements in *Gargantua and Pantagruel* was lost to view as the work (together with such parallel texts as Cervantes' *Don Quixote*) was relegated to the sidelines of the 'merely humorous'. Like the Formalists, Bakhtin thus recognizes that the function and effect of a particular literary text may vary according to the positions that it occupies within different 'literary systems'. The difference is that he understands this in a concrete sense and not merely abstractly. The effect of Rabelais' work is viewed not as an invariant one produced and guaranteed by the text itself but as a matter for concrete historical specification. It can only be calculated by taking into account the different political and ideological conjunctures which the text enters into during the course of its historical existence and the different ways in which that same text is 'worked' by the literary criticisms through which its reception is mediated.

Part Two

Marxist criticism: from aesthetics to politics

5

MARXISM VERSUS AESTHETICS

FORMALISM: A LOST HERITAGE

Bakhtin's study of Rabelais would seem fully to exemplify what a Marxist – that is, a historical and materialist – approach to the study of literary texts should look like. Remarkably free from the concerns of traditional aesthetics, it explains the distinguishing formal features of Rabelais' work not as the manifestation of some invariant set of uniquely distinguishing aesthetic properties but as the product of a particular, historically and materially constrained practice of writing. Furthermore, this 'materialism of production' is counterbalanced by a 'materialism of consumption' in the equally concrete and historically specific analysis Bakhtin offers of the different ways in which Rabelais' work has functioned and been recuperated within different ideological and political conjunctures. The question of a particular text's political effects, this suggests, cannot be resolved with reference to its formal properties, treated as an ahistorical abstraction, but requires an examination of the concrete and changing functions which that text fulfils in the real social process.

Although these achievements reflect a sustained critique of the Formalists' work and of the premises on which it rested, it is equally clear that, without the critical intervention made by the Formalists, these advances simply could not have been made. If Bakhtin's work defines and occupies a theoretical space that is situated 'beyond Formalism', that space was produced only by 'working through' Formalism. By taking both its claims and its problems seriously, Bakhtin was not only profoundly influenced by the Formalist heritage; he also *reorganized* that heritage, actively working upon and transforming Formalist concepts in the process of integrating them into his own theoretical concerns.

Bakhtin's concept of 'renewal', for example, is not merely a near-equivalent for the concept of defamiliarization – not a passive borrowing from Formalism on his part. It is a different concept, reflecting a process of theoretical work on and transformation of the concept of defamiliarization. It refers not to an invariant attribute which is felt to typify all so-called literary texts but to a particular formal effect wrought by European *belles lettres* during a particular stage in their historical development. Similarly, although taking over the Formalists' perception that the question of a text's function within a given 'literary system' cannot be resolved with reference to the conditions of its origin, Bakhtin gives this perception a more precise, a more materialist and historical formulation. Such changes in the effects and functions which it is possible to attribute to a text do not 'just happen' but are a product of the concrete ideological and political determinations which, through the mediation of criticism, operate on the text so as to condition its consumption.

There is, then, no need to 'call for' or 'invent' a dialogue between Formalism and Marxism. That dialogue has already taken place and, if our analysis is correct, was an extraordinarily productive one. Yet its impact on the mainstream of Marxist criticism has been negligible. The work of the Formalists, it is true, has exerted a marginal impact on Marxist criticism in recent years in the attempts of Marxist critics to come to terms with and incorporate the advances that have been made in structuralism and semiotics. The work of Roland Barthes and of other scholars associated with the journal *Tel Quel* has been most important in this respect. The general disillusionment with the political value of realist texts and, allied with this, a renewed interest in Brecht's work have also occasioned a renewed interest in the work of the Formalists. In particular, the concept of defamiliarization has proved an indispensable aid to theorizing the formal structure and effect of contemporary *avant-garde* literary practice. Important though these developments are, however, they reflect only a partial rediscovery of the Formalists, concerned solely with the contribution they have to make to our understanding of the formal devices which govern the construction of particular narrative structures or discourses. The broader philosophical and methodological concerns which formed the background to the Formalists' concern with such formal devices as part of an integrated theory of literariness have, by and large, been overlooked or, worse, dismissed as merely Kantian.

The situation with regard to Bakhtin is even more regrettable. With one or two exceptions, his works have been treated simply as exercises in 'practical criticism', little or no attempt having been made to quarry them for their theoretical yield.[1]

However, we will not dwell further on the reasons for this neglect here. Our aim in the second part of this study is to review some of the recent developments within Marxism which suggest that a dialogue between Formalist and Marxist criticism may again be undertaken with fruitful results. Our concern here will be with the work of Louis Althusser and with that of such critics as Pierre Macherey and Terry Eagleton who, although differing in particulars both from one another and from Althusser, can be generally said to share the same approach.

Briefly, we shall attempt to establish four different types of connection between this tradition and the work of the Formalists. First, we shall argue that the two approaches are *formally* similar with respect to the ways in which they respectively produce and define their 'object' – the concept of literature with which they work – and their concerns in relation to that object. Second, we shall argue that there is a degree of *substantive* similarity between the Formalists' position concerning the defamiliarizing nature of literary discourse and the argument of the Althusserians to the effect that 'literature' can be defined as a form of cognition whose uniqueness consists in its capacity to 'distance from within' the categories of dominant ideology. This entails, as a third level of connection, a similarity of *technique* in the respect that the detailed conceptual apparatus used by the Althusserians in order to dissect the formal operations of literary texts is closely modelled upon and clearly is influenced by the techniques of formal analysis developed by the Formalists. Finally, it will be argued that the two traditions are similar with respect to their *theoretical trajectories*. Both start off with a theory of 'literature' as such; both dissolve this essentially aesthetic concern in order to take account of the historical determinations which bear on both the text's production and its consumption.

We are not, however, interested in these parallels for their own sake. That would be a lame and, ultimately, purely formal undertaking. If we set out to contribute to a developing dialogue between Formalism and Marxism, to rediscover the lost heritage of Formalism, it is because we believe that this will be of positive assistance to Marxist criticism in enabling it to surmount some of the difficulties which currently face it. Of these, the need to sever the connection which has bound it to the concerns of bourgeois aesthetics, thereby impeding the realization of its historical and materialist ambitions, is perhaps the most pressing.

MARXIST CRITICISM: AESTHETICS, POLITICS AND HISTORY

Marxism has always claimed to be a revolutionary science. This means not merely that it is a science placed in the service of social and political revolution but also that it is, *as a science*, revolutionary in its approach to defining problems. Marx's thought, it is now generally recognized, constituted a genuine theoretical revolution in the history of economic, social and political thought. Instead of proposing new answers to the old problems that were pre-given in the traditional concerns of bourgeois political economy or philosophy, Marx displaced those concerns entirely by proposing a new set of questions: that is, a new 'problematic.'

The tradition of political philosophy which runs from Hobbes to Hegel, for example, regards the state as a political institution which is formed as the result of a series of contracts entered into between individual citizens and the sovereign power. The predominant concern of this tradition is, accordingly, with the duty of obedience individual citizens owe to the state and with the conditions under which, if the state violates the terms of the contract under which power is leased to it, this duty may be broken with. In Marx's writings on the state, these problems are simply not present but are instead replaced by a radically new set of problems: those concerning the state as an arena in which the conflicting interests of different classes are represented and fought out.

This notion of the 'theoretical break' between Marx's work and pre-Marxist forms of economic, social and political theory has played an important role in recent years – largely as a result of Althusser's work – in justifying Marxism's claim to be a specific science.[2] This 'theoretical break' was not, however, a once-and-for-all event which occurred simultaneously in all regions of Marxist theory. Whereas Marx himself cut the umbilical cord between his own economic theories and the bourgeois political economy from which he developed them, for example, it is frequently argued that Marxist political theory achieved a parallel independence only with Lenin's *The State and Revolution*.[3]

Marxists working in the sphere of ideology have had a much more difficult time of it. Although it is clear that a consistently Marxist approach to ideological and cultural forms must rest on historical and materialist premises, it has proved to be no easy task to forge the detailed theoretical and conceptual apparatus through which such an ambition might be realized. True, all Marxist approaches to these questions *claim* to be historical and materialist. But they too often turn out to be fatally contaminated by idealist categories that they have taken on board, almost unconsciously, from what have proved to be more developed and sophisticated schools of bourgeois cultural theory.

This is particularly true of Marxist literary criticism which, far from progressing by displacing the concerns of bourgeois aesthetics to produce a distinctively new set of problems, has been developed chiefly via a series of borrowings from the more developed and more available systems of bourgeois criticism and aesthetics. If the ambition of Marxist criticism is to be a science, one can only conclude that it is still in the stages of its 'ideological pre-history', firmly caught in an orbit around the concerns of bourgeois criticism and aesthetics from which it must one day detach itself it is to attain a genuine independence.

The reasons for this are many and complex. In part, it reflects the ambiguity of Marx's own writings on literary and artistic matters. Although he did not attempt to develop a systematic theory of art and literature, Marx did comment frequently and often at length on these matters.[4] Unfortunately, it is not always easy to reconcile what he has to say in these passages with the concerns and procedures embodied in the approach he took to the questions of economic and political analysis with which he was more centrally concerned. The question of the value that is to be placed on these writings is thus a vexed one that we cannot fully go into here.

It is quite clear, however, that the greater part of Marx's writings on art and literature, although penned by Marx, are in no sense indicative of the position of 'Marxism' on these matters. The 'theoretical break' which would inaugurate the development of Marxist criticism as a genuinely independent science is not located in Marx's work. The failure to recognize this uncomfortable fact and the correspondingly misplaced theoretical weight that has all too often been placed on Marx's writings in this area have formed a further impediment to the development of such a 'theoretical break'.

Perhaps more important, however, have been the circumstances in which the major schools of Marxist criticism were formed and developed. Perry Anderson has usefully distinguished two major phases in the history of Marxism which were of a crucial importance in this respect. The first consists of the second generation of Marxists – notably, Antonio Labriola, Franz Mehring, Karl Kautsky and Georgy Plekhanov – who assumed the intellectual leadership in the communist movement in the period immediately after the death of Marx and Engels and prior to the ascendency of Lenin and Trotsky. Anderson argues that, owing to the lull of revolutionary expectations which characterized this period, these theorists ceased to apply Marxism concretely and politically to the analysis of changing economic and political relationships. Instead, making Marxism itself the primary object of their attention, they sought 'to systematize historical materialism as a comprehensive theory of man and nature, capable of replacing rival bourgeois disciplines and providing the workers' movement with a broad and coherent vision of the world that could easily be grasped by its militants'.[5]

Although one should not underestimate the ideological value of this moment in the history of Marxism, its theoretical consequences were regrettable. For, in order to make Marxism compete with the traditional bourgeois disciplines, it was necessary to realign it with them, to make their concerns its concern also. By arguing that its categories could be applied to the pre-given problems, say, of philosophy or aesthetics and, moreover, that it could deal with these more successfully than its bourgeois counterparts, Marxism was thereby regarded as merely one school among others within these areas. Its claims to be revolutionary as a science were thus muted as it was made to provide new answers to old questions rather than to produce, within a theoretical space of its own making, an entirely new, incommensurable set of problems.

This tendency was repeated and exaggerated during the period of what Anderson calls 'western Marxism', running from Lukács' *History and Class Consciousness* (1925) to the present. 'The great wealth and variety of the corpus of writing produced in this domain,' Anderson writes of western Marxism's contribution to aesthetics, 'far richer and subtler than anything within the classical heritage of historical materialism, may in the end prove to be the most permanent collective gain of this tradition.'[6] This is true. Virtually all of the major theorists whose work defines this period – Georg Lukács, Walter Benjamin, Theodor Adorno, Herbert Marcuse, Lucien Goldmann, Jean-Paul Sartre, Galvano Della Volpe – have offered a major treatise on the contribution Marxism has to make to the study of literature. But it is equally true to say that these contributions, at least in part, reflect an unquestioning acceptance of the problems of traditional aesthetics as being ones with which Marxism should legitimately concern itself.

In this, western Marxism reflects the conditions of its genesis. The most distinctive feature of the period from 1925 onwards, Anderson argues, has been the virtually total severance of the link between theory and practice induced by the downturn of revolutionary expectations in western Europe and the subsequent economic and political consolidation of capitalism. All of the theorists whom we have cited were either, after an initial period of political involvement, divorced from concrete political pursuits, concerning themselves with theoretical issues in what was tantamount to a political vacuum (as was the case with Lukács), or, from the very beginning, had been concerned with Marxism in a purely theoretical sense (as was the case with Marcuse and Adorno). Furthermore, with the notable exception of Antonio Gramsci, they were all university professors writing about Marxism from within bourgeois or, in the case of Lukács, Stalinist academia.

Reflecting the impress of these constraints, the collective output of western Marxism amounts to a series of second-order discourses, 'on

Marxism, rather than in Marxism',[7] which have sought to reinterpret Marx's work by reviewing it in terms of categories of analysis supplied by some other theoretical or philosophical system. The various attempts that have been made to derive a Marxist aesthetic by relating Marx's work to the aesthetic theories of Hegel (Lukács) or Schiller (Marcuse) are indicative of this. The result is now a well-developed tradition of Marxist criticism which, although displaying a degree of conceptual sophistication and a mastery of both bourgeois literature and bourgeois aesthetics that can rival the best of bourgeois criticism, remains a commentary on, a critique of and an attempted incorporation of traditional aesthetics. It has failed to produce a new set of questions which would entirely supplant the concerns of pre-Marxist aesthetics.

In saying this, of course, we do not intend to speak dismissively of these traditions but merely to point to the price they have paid for being developed in such close proximity to the concerns of traditional aesthetics. The history of Marxist criticism is a history of two different sets of problems which have coexisted uneasily with one another. On the one hand, within the context of the topography of 'base' and 'superstructure' mapped out by Marx, there has been a sustained attempt to explain the form and content of literary texts by referring them to the economic, political and ideological relationships within which they are set. In addition, Marxist critics have always sought to calculate what sort of political effects might be attributed to literary works and, accordingly, to judge for or against different types of literary practice from stated political positions. On the other hand, with the possible exception of Brecht's work, every major phase in the development of Marxist criticism has been an enterprise in aesthetics. It has attempted to construct a theory of the specific nature of aesthetic objects and, within this, a theory of 'literature' as such.

Indeed, if there is a single dominant thread running through the history of Marxist criticism it is the attempt to reconcile these two sets of concerns: the one consistent with the historical and materialist premises of Marxism and with its political motivation, and the other inherited from bourgeois aesthetics. The crucial theoretical break lies in the recognition that, instead of 'Marxism *and* aesthetics', the real concern should be with 'Marxism *versus* aesthetics'. For it is not merely that these two concerns sit uncomfortably with one another. The inheritance of the conceptual equipment which goes with the concerns of aesthetics constitutes the single most effective impediment to the development of a consistently historical and materialist approach to the study of literary texts.

The latter concern requires one to focus on the *differences* between forms of writing, explaining these with reference to the differing, historically specific material and ideological constraints which have regulated their production. The former, by contrast, is concerned with the *similarities* between forms of writing. By abstracting particular texts from the historically specific circumstances of their production, it is argued that these can be grouped together as 'literature' precisely to the extent that they share some formal essence, some uniquely distinguishing set of formal properties, which marks them off from other, 'non-literary' forms of writing.

This formal essence, however it may be defined, does not figure merely as the principle of classification which justifies the 'literary'/ 'non-literary' distinction posited. It is also endowed with explanatory power as part of an idealist theory of causation. It is what *makes* the text concerned 'literary'. Far from being moulded by the circumstances of its production, the so-called 'literary' work is said to break free from these so as to partake of some universal, unchanging, ever-present formal essence. History may be allowed some explanatory power in relation to its peripheral features but, with regard to its essentially defining characteristics, the literary work is viewed as the manifestation of some universal, unchanging, always 'already there' ideal form which, so it is alleged, it merely realizes in a particular, contingent way.

To incorporate the concerns of aesthetics into Marxist criticism is thus necessarily to import into it a set of problems which can only be conceived in idealist terms. The result has been a mis-marriage as, more often than not, the materialist claims and ambitions of Marxist criticism have been decisively curtailed by the prior acceptance of a question – 'What is literature?' – which necessarily requires an idealist solution.

This is as true of the work of the Althusserians as of earlier traditions in Marxist criticism with the important qualification that, in its more recent developments, a genuine attempt has been made to effect the necessary theoretical revolution which will dislocate Marxist criticism from the concerns of aesthetics. We shall therefore, in the remainder of this study, try to follow the trajectory of these developments. In the case of Althusser, we shall show how the materialist ambition which underlies his approach to literature is effectively undercut by the idealist legacy he derives from bourgeois aesthetics. We shall then summarize the more recent work of Terry Eagleton and Pierre Macherey which, reflecting a conscious awareness of these problems, seeks to deal with them – not always successfully – in ways that reflect a more consistent historical and materialist approach to the questions of the production of literary texts and their political effects. First, however, we must indicate the processes by which this tradition has constituted its object – the concept of 'literature' with which it works and to which it addresses itself.

LITERATURE'S 'NON-SAID'

Most of the essential arguments here are contained in Pierre Macherey's *A Theory of Literary Production* (although they are rehearsed and extended in Eagleton's *Criticism and Ideology*) where the legitimate concerns of Marxist criticism are defined by juxtaposition with the two dominant forms of contemporary bourgeois criticism: structuralism and what Macherey calls *la critique comme appreciation*. As we have already indicated Macherey's position on the former, we shall concern ourselves solely with his objections to the latter.

La critique comme appréciation, or interpretative criticism, is, Macherey and Eagleton argue, inherently contradictory. Literary criticism sets out to deliver the text from its own silences by coaxing it into giving up its true, latent or hidden meaning, but can only do so by intruding its own discourse between the reader and the text. The more it seeks to enable the text to speak with its own voice – and the work of Leavis is a classic example in this respect – the more the voice of the critic obtrudes as the text is referred to an ideal or substitute text, elaborated by the critic, in relation to which the 'original' text is to be corrected, revised and, in general terms, tailored for consumption.

Such a criticism, then, effects a certain productive activity. It so 'works' the text, usually by smoothing out the contradictions within it, as to subject it to a particular, ideologically coded reading. But, at the same time, it effaces its own productive activity in presenting that reading as but the 'truth' of the text itself.

It is, ultimately, with the empiricist presuppositions of this form of criticism that Macherey and Eagleton take issue. The distinguishing feature of empiricism, Colin MacCabe has argued, consists 'in its characterization of the knowledge to be obtained as defined by the object of which it is knowledge'.[8] Empiricism, that is, consists in the belief that the object of knowledge is supposed to be somehow 'given' as a state of affairs, existing outside and independently of thought, which constitutes 'that which is to be known'. The process of knowledge is thus viewed as one through which, by a mixture of conceptual and empirical procedures, the 'is to be known' comes to be known, becomes the 'is known'. *La critique comme appréciation* thus constructs the text as if it had a pre-given hidden or true meaning which it is the business of criticism to 'come to know', to mirror in thought.

In opposition to this, Macherey proposes the concept of *la critique comme savoir*, of a criticism which produces its own 'text-for-criticism' through its own conceptual procedures and, in so doing, displays its productive activity on its sleeve. The process of science is not one whereby, through methodological and conceptual artifice, knowledge becomes, in the image of Faust, progressively more complete in relation to a pre-given reality which it mirrors. It is rather one in which, through the operations of science itself, reality is transformed into an object of knowledge that is produced, defined and pursued by exclusively theoretical means.

With regard to Marxist criticism, it is thus argued that its object is not the 'real object' constituted by the text as a pre-given entity. Nor should its aim be to arrive at a knowledge of what is already contained in the text, a reformulation of its 'already said'. Its aim should rather be to produce, as its 'text-for-criticism', the concept of the text's 'non-said': the process of the text's production. Marxist criticism must, as Eagleton puts it, aim to 'show the text as it cannot know itself, to manifest those conditions of its making (inscribed in its very letter) about which it is necessarily silent'[9] – an object which is not at all given or suggested by the text itself but which is produced solely by the analytical concerns of Marxism.

But what is this 'it' of which the text itself is silent and of which a knowledge is to be produced? For Macherey and Eagleton, the essence of a text's 'non-said' is its relationship to ideology and it is this – what may be described as the text's 'literary effect' – which is to be made the object of Marxist criticism. Literature, it is argued, is installed halfway between ideology and science and, through its formal mechanisms, it is said to work on the terms of seeing proposed by ideology so as to parody, invert or reveal them. Literature 'distances' ideology from within, affording a mode of access to the conditions of social existence which, whilst not providing a 'knowledge' of those conditions – the knowledge, that is, proposed by Marxism – reveals the 'misrecognition' of social relationships that is embodied in the ideology to which it alludes and from which, as 'literature', it detaches itself in the process of its production.

The central difficulty is that this concern is presented, at one and the same time, as both a historical and materialist concern and as a concern of aesthetics. According to the former, the promise is that of a science of literature which will reveal those mechanisms, inscribed within the literary text, which bring about the distancing of ideology that defines the 'literary effect' and which will explain the operation of such mechanisms with reference to the material and historical matrices of the text's production. This promise can only be achieved by construing such a 'literary effect' as being historically defined: that is, as the product of the formal properties of one form of writing that is distinguishable from others historically in terms of the forces and constraints which bear upon it.

This is a step which Eagleton seems always about to take, without ever quite doing so, and one which, in his most recent work, Macherey has recommended, albeit cryptically. This hesitation is explicable, ultimately, in terms of the legacy of aesthetics. For, side by side with the above historical tendency within the work of the Althusserians, there is also a tendency to define the 'literary effect' aesthetically as the result of some invariant set of formal properties which establish an eternal, ahistorical distinction between 'literary' works and other forms of writing. According to this strand within the argument, the ability of certain texts to work on and subvert the categories of dominant ideology appears not as the result of a historically particular practice of writing but as the manifestation of an eternally pre-given and forever unchanging literary essence. This tendency is most pronounced in the work of Althusser who, reflecting the traditionally close connection between aesthetics and epistemology, advances a theory of 'literature' as part of a general theory concerning the nature of the distinctions between science, literature and ideology which, in his view, stand as eternally separate and unchanging forms of our cognitive appropriation of reality.

6

SCIENCE, LITERATURE AND IDEOLOGY

ON PRACTICES

Althusser, we have seen, views a 'social formation' – a near equivalent of the sociological concept of 'society' – as consisting of a number of distinct but interrelated levels of 'practice' – the *economic*, the *political* and the *ideological* – each of which is relatively autonomous in relation to the others. The decisive concept here is that of 'practice':

> By *practice* in general I shall mean any process of *transformation* of a determinate given raw material into a determinate *product*, a transformation effected by a determinate human labour, using determinate means (of 'production').[1]

The basis for this argument is Althusser's conception of economic activity as 'the practice of the transformation of a given nature (raw material) into useful *products* by the activity of living men working through the *methodically organized* employment of determinate *means of production* within the framework of determinate relations of production'.[2] In referring to ideology as a 'practice' in this sense, Althusser thus proposes what might be described as a 'materialism of the superstructure'. Ideology is construed not as the pale, ethereal reflection of society's material base but as a practical *activity* which has its own, equally material means and relations of production and its own, equally material products. As a relatively autonomous level of the social formation, ideology is thus the product of quite specific determinants which are not reducible to economic relationships. Furthermore, as a material force, ideology wields a power all of its own in relation to the other levels of social practice.

So far, so good. The difficulty is that, within this general framework, Althusser seeks also to establish a series of distinctions between 'science' as such, 'literature' as such and 'ideology' as such. In differentiating between these as different forms of practice, each of which is said to work on and transform a given raw material into a determinate product characterized by a determinate 'effect' – the 'knowledge effect', the 'aesthetic effect' and the 'ideological effect' respectively – Althusser construes them as eternal and unchanging forms of cognition. The result of approaching the matter in this way is, effectively, a denial of the materialist premises from which Althusser sets out. Particular sciences, particular literary texts and particular ideological forms turn out to be not the result of materially conditioned practices so much as the mere manifestations of invariant structures.

ON IDEOLOGY

Althusser's theories concerning ideology are outlined mainly in two essays – 'Marxism and Humanism' (1965) and 'Ideology and Ideological State Apparatuses' (1969) – although it is the latter of these that has occupied the centre of the debate in view of the highly specific meaning it proposes for the concept of ideology.[3] For Althusser's concern in this essay is not with 'ideology' as a synonym for the concept of society's intellectual 'superstructure' comprising the totality of cognitive forms or signifying practices. He rather has in mind a concept of 'ideology' which refers to *one particular form of cognition* as the product of *one particular type of signifying practice.*

His argument is a difficult one, riddled with somewhat slippery and elusive concepts. Nevertheless, it can be summarized in six main propositions:

(i) *Ideology has a material existence.* Disputing the arguments advanced by Marx and Engels in *The German Ideology* according to which ideology is viewed as the inverted reflection, in thought, of real social relationships, Althusser argues that ideology has its own material existence. The ideas of a human subject, he maintains, exist only in his/her actions, and these actions are inserted into practices which are, in turn, 'governed by the *rituals* in which these practices are inscribed, within the *material existence of an ideological apparatus*',[4] such as a church, a school or a political rally. The celebration of communion might thus be regarded as quintessentially ideological. It consists of a practice of signification which, inscribed in ritual form and housed within the ideological apparatus of the church, produces the consciousness of the communicant: that is, produces him/her as, precisely, the subject of a religious consciousness.

More important than the insistence on the objective, material nature of ideology is the inversion of the traditional Marxist approach to the question of the social determination of consciousness which this involves. 'It is not men's consciousness that determines their being', Marx wrote, 'but, on the contrary, their social being that determines their consciousness.'[5] This implies that men's consciousness is to be explained as the product of the social relationships in which they live and of the particular positions which individuals or groups of individuals occupy in those relationships. Reversing the order of determination which this implies. Althusser contends that the consciousness of social individuals is organized and produced not by the place they occupy within the social structure but by the operations upon them of those material ideological forms which result from autonomous ideological practices operating from within autonomous ideological apparatuses. Far from being a mere reflex of a consciousness which is determined by class position, ideology is viewed as an autonomous level of production with its own product: namely, the consciousness of human subjects. The work that ideology effects is that of transforming individuals into concrete social beings who are the subjects of determinate forms of consciousness.

(ii) *Ideology functions so as to secure the reproduction of the relations of production.* Nicos Poulantzas has summarized the main point at issue here. The inner action of capitalist production and exchange, he argues, operates so as to reproduce the conditions of capitalist production. The completion of every cycle of exchange between capital and labour – that is, the transfer of expropriated surplus-value from the worker to capital – increases the dependency of the worker on capital at the same time as it increases the social power exerted by capital over the worker. In this way, the social relationship of wage labour which forms the basis of capitalist production is reproduced by the mechanisms at work within that relationship itself.

However, this economic process merely reproduces the *places* within the production process – wage-labourer, capitalist – that are to be occupied by the actual agents of production. There therefore remains, Poulantzas argues, the 'task of the reproduction and distribution of the agents themselves to these places':[6] that is, the allocation of different individuals to different positions within the production process and the production within those individuals of the capabilities and forms of consciousness and self-consciousness appropriate to the positions they occupy. Put simply, if capitalism is to survive as an ongoing system, then concrete social individuals must be reconciled both to the class structure and to the class positions within it which, as individuals, they occupy. They must be induced to 'live' their exploitation and oppression in such a way that they do not experience or represent to themselves their position as, precisely, one in which they are exploited and oppressed.

For Althusser, this work is carried out by the 'ideological state apparatuses': the education system, the media, the family, the church. What distinguishes these from the normal apparatuses of state power – the police, the army – is that, whereas the latter function by coercion or the threat of coercion, the 'ideological state apparatuses' 'function "by ideology"'.[7] By this Althusser does not mean merely that such apparatuses provide the location within which the business of the production of consciousness is actually organized and carried out. Nor does he mean simply that their concern is to effect a willing or passive compliance which will reduce the need for active coercion. He more particularly means that these apparatuses function by 'ideology' as such in the sense that the practices they produce and transmit conform to an invariant structure which induces in those who are subjected to its action an 'imaginary' (and, by implication, 'false') relationship to the conditions of their existence.

(iii) *Ideology has no history.* This next step is decisive. Arguing that an understanding of particular ideologies can only be constructed on the basis of a theory of 'ideology in general', Althusser contends that, whilst particular ideologies have a history which is, in part, determined by historical forces situated outside themselves, 'ideology' in itself has no history. In other words, there is present in all particular, historically determined ideologies an unchanging structure which is said to typify 'ideology' as such. The primary task of the theory of ideology is thus that of describing the structure which regulates not particular ideologies but the timeless totality of 'ideology' itself, an eternal, forever pre-given structure which overarches all the variant, historically determined, concrete forms of ideological practice in which it is manifested. For it is always by means of the operation of this invariant structure that particular ideological practices fulfil their allotted function of organizing individuals into 'subjects'.

(iv) *All ideology hails or interpellates concrete individuals as concrete subjects, by the functioning of the category of the subject.* The structure of 'ideology' as such is 'subject centred'. It contains at its centre the concept of a Unique or Absolute Subject, capable of serving as the guarantor of His own meaningfulness – the concept of God in Christian theology, for example, or of Man in bourgeois philosophical humanism. This Unique or Absolute Subject 'recruits', 'hails', or 'interpellates' concrete individuals into concrete subjects. Although the argument is complex, the gist of it is that the concept of such an Absolute Subject acts as the focal point of identification whereby individuals are organized into subsidiary 'subjects': that is, into socially formed subjects of consciousness who regard themselves as having an identity, a role and a part to play within a process – theological or historical – which has a sense, direction and meaning conferred on it by the Absolute Subject. Ideology might thus be said to consist of those myths through which individuals are reconciled to their given social positions by falsely representing to them those positions and the relationships between them as if they formed a part of some inherently significant, intrinsically coherent plan or process.

(v) *Ideology is a 'representation' of the imaginary relationship of individuals to their real conditions of existence.* It is by virtue of the operation of this subject-centred structure, then, that ideology produces within individuals a purely 'imaginary' relationship to the real conditions of their social existence. The 'effect' of ideology is thus one of 'misrecognition'. It does not represent to men either the real nature of the conditions of their existence or the real nature of their relationship to those conditions. On the contrary, ideology proposes an entirely 'imaginary' and, by implication, false representation of individuals' relationship to the conditions of their existence which, in being taken for granted, constitutes the form in which people 'live' (as in Ortega y Gasset's sense) their relationship to those conditions.

The effect of the classical forms of bourgeois humanism, for example, is such that the bourgeois 'lives' his relationship to the conditions of social existence not on the basis of a 'knowledge' of his objective class position in the relationships of production. His perception of his place in the social world is, rather, mediated through an entirely 'imaginary' construction of his own role, and that of his class, in a historical process which is represented as having a logic, a sense and a direction as a series of developmental sequences through which Man's essential nature is progressively realized. The bourgeois thus 'lives' or represents to himself his relationship to the conditions of existence not as an exploiting capitalist but as an instrument of History.

(vi) *Ideology is as such an organic part of every social totality.* Finally, 'ideology' as such is 'indispensable in any society', including that of a fully developed communism, 'if men are to be formed, transformed and equipped to respond to the demands of their conditions of existence'.[8] This means that, in communist society too, ideology will continue to operate through the category of the 'subject' and that its function will continue to be that of adjusting and reconciling individuals to the positions they occupy in the process of production.

Ideology, then, is regarded as a practice which works on the raw material of social relationships with the instruments of ideological production provided by its subject-centred structure. In so doing, it transforms those relationships into representations of 'imaginary' relationships to them which, defining the terms in which we 'live' our relationship to the conditions of our social existence, induce in us a 'misrecognition' of those conditions. Individuals are related, in ideology, to the conditions of their existence through the imaginary concept of their own selfhood and of the place they occupy within 'the order of things' as governed over and given sense and coherence by the Absolute Subject of God, Man, Nation, etc.

We can already see the tension between the historical and materialist and the idealist concepts at work in Althusser's writings. On the one hand, ideology is viewed as a practice, the product of a real, materially constrained process of production. On the other hand, its product is always 'already there' as an invariant structure to which, it would seem, all ideologies must inevitably conform. This tension is ultimately reducible to the fact that Althusser makes the term 'ideology' do too much. In one usage it refers to a particular type of practice which produces in men and women a particular type of mental relationship to the conditions of their existence. According to its other usage, however, it functions as an epistemological concept. In being opposed to science it stands for the simple opposite of Truth as an eternal and abstract category.

ON SCIENCE

A similar tension is evident in his theory of science. On the one hand, science is viewed as a practice which works on and transforms the raw material provided by prevailing ideologies by bringing to bear upon them the instruments of theoretical production – that is, the distinctive concepts – which characterize that science. This whole process of transformation, furthermore, is set within the context of socially determined relations of theoretical production. On the other hand, the structure of the system of scientific thought which results from this process of transformation is something that is 'already there', a pre-formed essence which is not at all determined by the process of that science's making.

Althusser thus argues that the structure of 'science' as such is defined by its 'subjectlessness' as a form of discourse. He seems to use this concept in several different ways. First, science is 'subjectless' in the sense that it is only the impersonal 'one' that can serve as the subject of 'knowledge'. In science, what is 'known' is known impersonally; 'knowledge' cannot be attributed to the subject 'I'. Second, scientific knowledge is subjectless in the sense that it 'is the historical result of a process which has no real subject or goals'.[9] Science has no ultimate end or *telos*. Nor is there any subject to which it can be attributed. Crucially, it cannot be viewed as a unitary process tending toward a final state in which Man's knowledge – Man, here, serving as the subject of predication for 'knowledge' – will be complete.

Third and most distinctively, however, science is distinguishable from other forms of cognition by the fact that it imposes a 'subjectless' system of representation on the world. Althusser argues that it is in this sense that Marx transformed Hegel's concept of history. Whereas Hegel conceived of history as an evolutionary process which is governed over, given sense and coherence by the concept of Spirit, Marx is said to have developed the concept of history as a 'process without a subject'.[10] Historical change, that is, depends, for Marx, on the ways in which the real determinations of class contradiction work themselves out. As such, history has no foreseeable end or goal, no intrinsic sense or direction as was traditionally guaranteed by subject-centred philosophies or religions. Just as Galileo freed the orbit of the planets from the pull of geocentric conceptions, so Marx freed the real determinants of historical development – class struggle – from anthropomorphizing or spiritualizing conceptions.

Finally, as the product of a theoretical practice, science is characterized by its 'knowledge effect'. This is not to say that science is true in the sense of conforming to 'reality' but that a science opens up a new conceptual space, a new continent of knowledge (in Marx's case, the continent of history) of which a knowledge *is to be produced*. Paradoxically, science is distinguishable from ideology not by what it 'knows' but by what it opens up as a possible *object* of knowledge, by its *production* of problems in contradistinction to ideology's effect of reducing them: of limiting inquiry by advancing claims of false knowledge. Marx thus made the study of history scientific, not because he claimed to know the 'truth' of history as had earlier philosophies of history, but, precisely the opposite, because he made history problematic.[11]

ON ART AND LITERATURE

Although primarily concerned with the relationship between science and ideology, Althusser has sketched out the implications of his position for the way in which art and literature should be viewed in three essays: 'The "Piccolo Teatro": Bertolazzi and Brecht' (1962), 'A Letter on Art' (1966) and 'Cremonini, Painter of the Abstract (1966).[12] It is clear from these that what Althusser has in mind is the development of a theory of 'literature' as such in parallel with his theory of 'ideology' as such and of 'science' as such. Construing 'literature' as an unchanging structure which, pre-existing above and beyond the variant concrete forms in which it is manifested, gives rise to an invariant 'aesthetic effect', Marxist criticism is assigned the task of producing a knowledge of the processes by which this 'effect' is produced:

> As you can see, in order to answer most of the questions posed for us by the existence and specific nature of art, we are forced to produce an adequate (scientific) *knowledge* of the processes which produce the 'aesthetic effect' of the work of art.[13]

A knowledge of art and literature, then, is to complete the 'trilogy of the superstructure' consisting of practices which give rise to different types of cognitive appropriation of reality. We can see here just how much of the legacy of aesthetics is unquestioningly taken on board by Althusser. That 'art' exists and has a specific nature is simply taken for granted. Furthermore, in simply subsuming 'literature' under the general category of 'art', it is clear that what is being sought is some 'effect' which all art forms might be said to share in spite of the fact that they differ both in material form and in respect of the relations of production within which, as different artistic practices, they are set. To put the objection simply: why should there be any common features shared by poetry, novel writing, painting, sculpture, music and drama which would justify our regarding them as 'art' in this sense? In failing to ask this question – and to ask this question is the only means of breaking with the concerns of aesthetics – Althusser simply assumes that there is some such set of common features which must be described and analysed.

Given this, the specificity of art is said to consist in the essentially mid-way, equivocal position it occupies between science and ideology. 'Art' *as such* hovers between 'science' *as such* and 'ideology' *as such*. Whilst it does not form 'knowledge' in the strict sense, art – 'authentic art', that is, 'not works of an average or mediocre level'[14] – is said to occupy a special relationship to science in that it enables us to 'see', 'perceive' or 'feel' something that alludes to reality. That 'something' is 'the ideology from which it is born, in which it bathes, from which it detaches itself as art, and to which it *alludes*'.[15]

Althusser, then, 'does not rank art among the ideologies'.[16] To the contrary, 'real art' is a practice which, using instruments of production of its own, works on and transforms the raw material provided by ideology to produce, not the 'knowledge effect' of science but the 'aesthetic effect' of 'making visible' (donner à voir), by establishing a distance from it, the reality of the existing ideology,[17] transfixing it so that we might see its operations at work. Art and literature do not deal with a sphere of reality peculiar to themselves. The object on which they work and which they transform is 'the spontaneous "lived experience" of ideology, in its peculiar relationship to the real'.[18] But this, Althusser argues, is also an object of science – by which, in this context, he *means* (but does not *say*) the Marxist science of ideology:

> The real difference between art and science lies in the *specific form* in which they give us the same object in quite different ways: art in the form of 'seeing' and 'perceiving' or 'feeling', science in the form of *knowledge* (in the strict sense, by concepts).[19]

Literature, then, 'gives us' ideology in a way that is different from the knowledge of its objective class function as proposed by Marxism. It enables us, in a vocabulary which recalls that of Shklovsky, to 'see', 'perceive' or 'feel' it. In Shklovsky's terms, it bestows a perceptibility on ideology, returning it from 'recognition' to 'seeing' by 'foregrounding' its operations.

How does it do this? In part, by working on and turning out habituated ideological forms including, in this sense, previous literary or dramatic forms. In this sense, Althusser's position is virtually indistinguishable from that of the Formalists. In a more specific sense, however, art and literature are said to attain their 'aesthetic effect' by virtue of their ability to 'decentre' the concept of the Absolute Subject which, as we have seen, constitutes the focal point of identification within any ideology. In so doing, they disrupt the 'imaginary' forms through

which individuals' relationship to the conditions of their social existence is represented to them.

It is in this sense that Althusser refers to Brecht's *Mother Courage* as a
'decentred totality'. For what it effects, he argues, is a 'decentring' of
bourgeois humanist ideology by displacing the Subject of Man which
is at its centre with an interrogation of the real conditions of existence.
The *true* centre of *Mother Courage*, he argues, is not its *apparent* centre –
Mother Courage herself as a 'stand-in' for the Absolute Subject of Man
and His Suffering – but the real conditions of war which are responsible for the loss of her children. Through the Brechtian devices of
'alienation', the audience is inhibited from empathizing with Mother
Courage's plight and, instead, is directed toward an examination of the
conditions of war responsible for that plight. Or, more accurately, it is
Mother Courage's behaviour itself that the audience is invited to scru-
tinize. In distancing us from Mother Courage's stoical acceptance of
her own suffering, Brecht enables us to 'see', 'perceive' or 'feel' the
ideological forms of bourgeois humanism which lie behind that sto-
icism and which mediate and condition Mother Courage's response to
her trials. Through a literary transformation enacted upon them, the
ideological forms of bourgeois humanism are thus ruptured from
within. They are, in Formalist parlance, 'foregrounded' in the character
of Mother Courage herself.

A parallel example is provided by Pierre Macherey's analysis of Jules
Verne's works. These, Macherey argues, are characterized by a contradiction between what he calls the level of *figuration* and that of *representation*, between the 'what is said' or, if you like, the story-line, and the
way in which the story is formally manipulated by the workings of the
text – a distinction which recalls that proposed by Shklovsky between
the concepts of *fabula* and *sjuzet*. With regard to the former of these
levels, Macherey argues that the story-lines of Verne's works 'reflect'
the ideology of the colonizing French bourgeoisie during the Third
Republic. Verne's works, that is, invariably concern the domination of
Nature by Man as a linear project that is nearing completion. This
project is expressed in the figure of the 'straight line' of the adventures
of his heroes who surmount the obstacles, human and natural, placed
in the path of their will to penetrate to and dominate one of nature's
extremities (the centre of the earth, the moon, the bottom of the sea).

This is how the ideological theme, the project of a colonizing bourgeoisie, 'tells itself'. And we can see how, through the workings of such
an ideology, the bourgeoisie 'lives' its relationship to colonialism. It
does so not on the basis of a knowledge of its objective economic and
political causes and effects but through an entirely imaginary form in
which, 'interpellated', 'called' or 'hailed' by the Absolute Subject of
Man, the individual bourgeois represents to himself his position in
the process of colonization as part of an inherently meaningful and
cumulative historical process.

Macherey's point is that, as embodied in the texture of Verne's
works, this ideological theme is not 'told' in this way but is rather 'told'
in a way that limits it and reveals it as ideology. He thus points out that
the project of exploration in Verne's works always turns out to be a
voyage of rediscovery as his heroes, believing themselves to be at the
forefront of Man's conquest of Nature, always find that they are following the path of one who has gone before them and has already arrived at
the destination they believed they would be the first to reach: the role of
Arne Saknussem in *Journey to the Centre of the Earth*, for example. Nature's
extremities, in other words, prove always to be already occupied, just as
did the countries which were on the receiving end of France's colonizing mission. In thus 'working' the ideology of the colonizing bourgeoisie so as to catch it, as it were, with its pants down; in 'decentring'
the concept of Man which constitutes its focal point of identification,
Verne's works could be said to have called into question the illusions
through which the bourgeoisie falsely represented to itself its colonizing ventures as part of a historic mission undertaken on the part of
humanity. For they constantly, if obliquely, draw attention to that part
of humanity that was excluded from the equation: the 'natives'.

Macherey does not, of course, suggest that the significance of
Verne's works is limited to their relationship to late nineteenth-century
French colonial ideology. Indeed, he treats the latter as but a particular
manifestation of a more general, West European ideological formation
– best exemplified by the Robinson Crusoe legend – which, he argues,
masked the real nature of the history of colonialism. That history was
falsely represented in the form of a myth of genesis, as a 'new history'
created on virgin territory through the triumphant application of
science and industry. Verne does not, Macherey argues, oppose this

myth of origin by recording the real history of colonization. Nor does his work simply 'reflect' the contradictions which are latently inscribed within the ideology. For, in Macherey's definition, ideologies are internally coherent, non-contradictory wholes. They do not contain any contradictions which can be simply 'reflected' in other practices. They can only be *put into* contradiction by practices which work on them from without. This, Macherey contends, is what Verne's works do by showing that the origin of the Crusoe myth is a false origin, a beginning which always presupposes the real history it suppresses.

In thus acting as an *agent-provocateur* in the midst of ideology, silently nudging it into a betrayal of itself, the 'effect' of literature might be construed as inherently critical. In temporarily prising apart the chains of ideology, it creates a kind of open, disengaged mental space within which a new attitude to reality might be produced. Literature does not produce a revolutionary consciousness. Nor does it replace ideology with scientific knowledge. But it does induce a temporary suspension of ideology, a temporary release from its operations, which may give rise to a new form of attentiveness to and thoughtfulness about reality.

Of course, it is not pretended that all works of literature distance ideology with the same degree of explicitness as do Brecht's. Nor is it argued that, in the exchange between 'literature' and 'ideology' as enacted within the literary text, it is always the former that has the last word. To the contrary, it is made clear in Macherey's work that, having been 'opened up' by the operations of the literary text, ideology reasserts itself within the text itself, sealing the holes which have been made within it by effecting its own recuperation of the literary trans- formations which distance it. Nevertheless, although fundamentally ambivalent, caught in a two-way movement from ideology and back to it again, literature, to a greater or lesser degree, 'rocks' the solidity of ideology, revealing its fault-lines or fissures.

Indeed, this critical effect *could be* viewed as a *necessary function* which is mapped out for literature within Althusser's 'trilogy of the super- structure'. For it is viewed not merely as a form of cognition that is mid-way between science and ideology but also as a kind of half- way staging house on the road which leads the individual from the 'misrecognition' of ideology in which s/he is always spontaneously trapped to the 'knowledge' of science.[20]

7

THE LEGACY OF AESTHETICS

THE LESSONS OF FORMALISM

We should, at this point, stress that Althusser is not primarily a literary critic. He has dealt with matters of literary theory more or less *en passant* purely in order to sketch out the implications of his more general theoretical position for this area of debate within Marxism. Nevertheless, his comments on literature have assumed a more than ordinary importance. Although they do not amount to a developed and sustained theoretical position in themselves, they do provide the general theoretical background against which the more detailed work of Pierre Macherey and Terry Eagleton must be viewed.

As we move to criticize Althusser, we should also stress that our concern is not to bite the hand that has been the source of so much theoretical nourishment in recent years. On the positive side, the outstanding contribution of Althusser's work, especially when viewed against the concerns of reflection theory, is that it has enabled us to 'think' the literary text as a practice of transformation, as a working upon and transforming of other forms of representation which gives rise to distinctive 'effects' whose social impact can be subjected to a political calculation. The difficulty is that, having theorized 'science' and 'ideology' epistemologically as universal and invariant forms of cognition, Althusser was forced to theorize 'literature' aesthetically as an equally universal and invariant form of our mental appropriation of reality. The result is that, although literature is viewed as a process of the productive transformation of other forms of cognition, the process of its production can never in fact be conceptualized. Equally, its political effects can be calculated only in an abstract, transhistorical fashion.

We might discover the reasons for this by considering further the similarities between Althusser's position and that of the Formalists. For both theorize the specific nature of literature as a practice of transformation enacted on forms of cognition which, in one way or another, are held to condition our habitual perceptions of the social world. Literary works, in both cases, are held to effect a 'work' on such habituated forms of cognition which, so to speak, turns them inside-out, revealing the stitch-work by which they are held together.

In both cases, then, it is a *relationship of transformation* that is placed at the centre of study. Furthermore, this relationship is understood to be inscribed within the structure of the literary text itself and to be analysable in the interplay between the different levels of discourse which comprise it. We have thus seen that, for the Formalists, two orders are constantly visible in the literary work: the established literary canon and the artistic novelty as a deviation from that canon. In a similar way, according to the Althusserian formulation and as stressed by Eagleton at great length, the ideology on which the text works is present in the text as one level within it, constantly pressing against and resisting the literary devices which limit it.

According to both the Formalists and the Althusserians, then, the literary text affords a triple structure of vision. First, it offers a vision of the habituated forms on which it works, casting them in a new light by virtue of the transformation to which it subjects them. Second, and in so doing, the literary text prises 'reality' away from the terms of reference which normally condition our access to the social world and thus produces a perception of new or unexpected aspects of that world. Finally, the literary text offers a vision of its own formal operations, revealing itself as the product of a transformation in the disjunction or tension between the two levels – the 'literary' and the 'ideological' – which account for its real complexity.

Where the two approaches most obviously differ is with respect to the nature of the 'raw materials' which literature is said to work on and transform. For the Formalists, the prevailing literary canons or, in the case of poetry, the conventionalized relationship between signifier and signified within the structure of *la langue* are the prime candidates in this respect. Neither these nor the effect produced by the literary transformations to which they are subjected are viewed in terms of their political consequences within the framework of a general theory of ideology. For Althusser, by contrast, the forms which literature works on and subverts are held to be conditioned by the architechtonic structure of 'ideology' and, therefore, to have an objective political role within the social process. This distinction is most clearly visible in Eagleton's *Criticism and Ideology* where it is argued – in terms that reflect a symbiosis of Formalist and Althusserian categories – that literature works on and transforms the 'signifier' of ideology and the 'signified' of history. Literature does not merely dissolve the bond between form and meaning which attaches a particular signifier to a particular signified in an abstract and neutral sense. It dissolves that particular bond of form and meaning which is placed on history by ideology. And it does so by means of the formal devices through which it 'foregrounds' the operations of that ideology.

Beneath these similarities, however, there is one further crucial difference. The Formalists did not merely theorize the relationships of transformation inscribed within the literary text. They also theorized the concept of 'literary function'. And they did not confuse the two. The question as to whether a given text fulfilled the function of defamiliarization required by the concept of literariness depended not solely on its formal properties but on the relationships which those properties established for that text within a given cultural field. In speaking of 'literature' in this way, the Formalists had in mind not a thing with an *essence* – a fixed and congealed set of texts whose literary function is forever ordained by their formal properties – but a *relationship* and a *function* which may be fulfilled or realized in different ways by different texts according to the changing historical relationships between texts which result from the organization of different 'literary systems'.

This is, admittedly, still an abstract formulation. For it presents the function of literariness as being forever pregiven and suggests that there must always and necessarily be certain forms of writing which are capable of fulfilling this function in every society. In thus representing literariness as an eternal, abstract, unchanging function capable of being contingently realized in different ways, the Formalists remained prisoners of aesthetics. Nevertheless, their position was more historical than Althusser's for it enabled them to refrain from drawing any permanent, irrevocable line between one set of written texts that might be regarded as 'literary' and other forms of writing. The line they drew was one between two different *functions* – the literary function of defamiliarization and the non-literary function of recognition. The same text may thus possibly shift from one side of this line to the other according to both the point from which it is viewed within the history of writing and the different systems of intertextual relationships into which it enters during its history as a received text.

This crucial ability to 'think' the variability of the text's function and effect is entirely absent from Althusser's construction of 'literature' and 'ideology' as invariant structures which eternally face one another across an equally eternal epistemological gap. By theorizing the specificity of 'literature' in these terms, Althusser's materialism is truncated at the point of both his analysis of the production of literature and his calculation of its political effects.

A NEW IDEALISM

It has been pointed out that the analytical topography of Marxism demands that, in some sense, 'superstructural' forms should be explained with reference to the social and material constraints which bear on their production. Althusser's concept of 'practice' theoretically allows one to do this in a way that is not liable to the charge of reductionism. Whilst admitting the determining role of the economy, it does so without denying the role of autonomous determinants unique to the ideological level of social practice. Further, it construes 'practice' as an active process of transformation, resulting in the production of cultural forms that are entirely new and unexampled. This promise, however, is denied by the idealist legacy of aesthetic and epistemological categories. Far from being genuinely the product of particular, materially conditioned practices, particular sciences, particular ideologies and particular works of literature inevitably conform to invariant structures that are eternally pre-given to them.

As a result, 'practice' turns out to be a redundant category. Or, more accurately, it is conceived as a teleological process of the adjustment of the real to the ideal. It is a ghostly process in the sense that its product is always 'already there' as a formal essence which governs the constitutive features of any science, any ideology or any work of literature quite irrespective of the historically concrete processes of their making. In the last analysis, it is not real, concrete individuals who are the subjects of practice, but abstract structures. The work of transformation that is effected in the interchange between a particular literary text and a particular ideology is, in effect, the work of one abstract structure on another. Behind every particular process of literary transformation, the disembodied gladiators of 'literature' and 'ideology' are locked in an eternal combat and, so far as Althusser is concerned, it is here that the real struggles take place.

We must, then, jettison the epistemological ballast of Althusser's theory. For if it is to be argued that there is an invariant structure which defines 'literature' as a form of cognition which is distinguishable epistemologically from science and ideology as unchanging forms of our mental appropriation of reality, then Marxism is confronted with what must, from a materialist point of view, be a paradox: namely, that this invariant structure is the product of practices of writing which differ from one another quite markedly with reference to the concrete historical and material determinants which underlie their production. How can such a unanimity of 'effect' result from such a plurality of 'causes'? Clearly, one can answer such a question only by resurrecting idealist categories: by suggesting that the structure which is manifested in such texts is eternally present as an ideal force moulding the practices through which it eventually realizes itself in variant concrete forms.

The only alternative is to argue that, if certain forms of writing do indeed display a tendency to rupture the categories of certain ideological forms from within, then this is the result of a conduct of the practice of writing that is distinguished from others not aesthetically but historically. This implies that other forms of writing – including major as well as minor forms – may display different forms of relationship to the dominant ideologies with which, historically, they are coeval. What is needed is not a theory of literature *as such* but a historically concrete analysis of the different relationships which may exist between different forms of fictional writing and the ideologies to which they allude.

This may not be so neat as an all-encompassing aesthetic. But it does have the merit of enabling one to come to terms with the full variety of cultural practice without constraining one's inquiries within the straitjacket of unworkable aesthetic and epistemological categories. If we interpret the concept of 'literature' extensively to refer to all forms of writing, and if we go beyond the parameters of the received tradition – comprised, by and large, of the *belles lettres* of the bourgeois epoch – to include not only medieval literature but the literature of ancient China and that of feudal Japan, not to mention the vast range of contemporary writing which customarily goes under the heading of either 'mass' or 'popular' culture, we confront a range and variability of writing which cannot be compressed within a single formula no matter how liberally it is interpreted. Althusser's mistake is that, although in fact concerned with bourgeois *belles lettres*, he misleadingly equates them with 'literature' as such. By thus falsely abstracting bourgeois *belles lettres* from the historical matrices of their production, he 'misrecognizes' their specific nature by construing and explaining it in aesthetic instead of historical terms.

Equally important, the production of that ideological or cultural space within which certain texts may take on a 'literary' function or effect (however this is defined) is itself something that needs to be explained. This involves a consideration of the determinations which work upon the text, once it has been produced, in order so to establish its relationships to other texts that it is, by the practices which work on it, produced for consumption as, precisely, 'literature'.

This is not a problem for Althusser. To 'answer the question of the relationship between art and knowledge', Althusser writes, 'we must produce a *knowledge of art*.'[1] But this is to assume that there is a something called 'art' of which a knowledge is to be produced. As Macherey has subsequently argued, the related question – 'What is literature?' – is a false question:

Why? Because it is a question which already contains an answer. It implies that literature is *something*, that *literature* exists as a *thing*, as an eternal and unchangeable *thing* with an essence.[2]

Althusser, explaining the process of literary production in idealist terms, compounds this error by cocooning the literary text, once produced, from the further irruptions of history. Literature's effect – aesthetic or political – would seem to be a given, the invariant and necessary product of its purely formal properties. If the effect of ideology is, by definition, that of a 'misrecognition' of social relationships and if the 'knowledge effect' of science – of Marxist science – is, by definition, revolutionary in the sense that it undercuts dominant ideological representations, then literature would seem to be necessarily 'critical', 'radical' or 'progressive' in its effect by virtue of its capacity to rupture ideological forms from within. If science is always on the side of the angels whilst ideology speaks always for the devil, literature, straddled mid-way between the two, symbolizes the human predicament: capable of denouncing the devil and his works but, at the same time, denied the light of Truth.

But, as Marx reminds us often enough, it is only consumption which completes the process of production. Whilst the literary text may, by virtue of its intrinsic properties, determine to a certain extent the way in which it is 'consumed' or read, it does not do so entirely. For the process of the consumption of literary texts is necessarily that of their continuous re-production; that is, of their being produced as different objects for consumption. This is not merely to say that the history of criticism is one of 'creative treason' whereby the same texts are successively plundered for different meanings. The way in which the literary text is appropriated is determined not only by the operations of criticism upon it but also, and more radically, by the whole material, institutional, political and ideological context within which those operations are set.

The Formalists argued, as we have seen, that the value and function of a text cannot be read off from the circumstances of its origin but depend on its position in the different systems of relationships between texts into which it is inscribed during different moments of its historical existence. Similarly, the political effects of a text cannot be read off from its relationship to the ideology which, during the process of its production, that text works upon and transforms. As Francis Mulhern has argued:

> What a text 'shows' or can be made to show of its means of production is of incontestable importance. But it cannot be decisive, either theoretically or in the 'politics' of criticism. Firstly, because, if a text is not an 'event' but a 'function' transposable in time and space, its conditions of *production* can have no special priority in analysis over its subsequent and variable conditions of *existence and activity*. Secondly, because what the entire history of discourse on literature shows is how much, in how many different circumstances, a text can be made to signify; what has to be confronted in bourgeois criticism is not only the ideological import of its practices but the fact of its *results*: an infinite variety of interpretations and judgements, all grounded more or less unimpeachably in 'the words on the page'.[3]

Two things follow from this. First, the political effects of literary texts must be calculated not abstractly but in relation to the historically concrete and varying modes in which they are appropriated. There can be no complete, final, once-and-for-all assessment of the political value of literary works. The attempt to make an eternal political value out of realism, as undertaken by Lukács, or to make out that the disruptive forms of contemporary *avant-garde* literary practice are intrinsically radical in their effect: these and other such ahistorical systems of political evaluation are mistaken in principle. In history, nothing is intrinsically 'literary', intrinsically 'progressive' or, indeed, intrinsically anything. If production is completed only with consumption, then, so far as literary texts are concerned, their production is never completed. They are endlessly *re-produced*, endlessly remade with different political consequences and effects and it is this, the position of the text within the full material social process that must be made the object of inquiry.

It might, for example, be argued that Shakespeare's *Macbeth* critically explores the torsions and limits of nascent bourgeois individualism. But this tells us nothing about the role and function of Shakespeare's work in our own society. Such matters can only be raised by examining the concrete mediating forces which currently bear on Shakespeare's work. This would require that we examine the way in which Shakespeare's texts are used within schools, the way in which they are appropriated by the 'culture industry' at large, their place within the theatre and the social role and function of the theatre itself. Furthermore, such an analysis could not be a neutral, purely scientific undertaking. One can calculate the political effects of a literary text only from the viewpoint of a given stated political position. In today's political arena, for example, the strategic dictates of Eurocommunism give rise to one set of literary-political calculations whereas those of an intransigent proletarianism give rise to another. There is and can be no neutral, scientifically validated ground which can assert the correctness of one of these positions over and against the other.[4]

Second, it follows that the activity of criticism is itself a preeminently *political* exercise. For the texts on which Marxist criticism works are, in a sense, already 'occupied'. They are already filled with interpretations. The way in which they are appropriated is already determined by the uses to which they are put in the social process. Given this, the quest for an objective 'science' of the literary text is illusory. The literary text has no single or uniquely privileged meaning, no single or uniquely privileged effect that can be abstracted from the ways in which criticism itself works upon and mediates the reception of that text. In this sense, literature is not something to be studied; it is an area to be occupied. The question is not what literature's political effects *are* but what they might be *made to be* – not in a forever and once-and-for-all sense but in a dynamic and changing way – by the operations of Marxist criticism. Perhaps the most important charge that can be laid against Althusser's work is that he exiles politics from his own criticism and, ultimately, from literature itself.

CRITICISM AND POLITICS

Althusser's concept of 'literature' is perhaps most vulnerable precisely because its stability depends on its relationship to the concepts of 'science' and 'ideology'. If anything were to call into doubt either of these definitions, then the concept of 'literature' would be thrown into acute crisis. Yet this is precisely what has happened. Althusser's assertions concerning the relationship between ideology and science have been so damagingly criticized that it is now clear that they are untenable.

Fortunately, it is not necessary to rehearse this debate in its entirety as Jacques Rancière's objections will take us to the heart of the matter.[5] Althusser's mistake, Rancière argues, was to generalize the distinction between Marxist science and those systems of ideas which it regards as ideological into an opposition between science and ideology in general. Regarding ideology as the Other of science, facing and sustaining its opposite in a mirror definition of Truth and Falsehood, Althusser further construed this opposition as an inherently *class* opposition. Rather than conceiving of particular ideologies, particular works of literature and particular sciences which, according to their nature and the uses to which they are put, may be either progressive or regressive in their political implications, each being mapped out as an area of class struggle, Althusser's position implied that class struggle takes place between the eternal verities of science, the eternal falsehoods of ideology and the eternal equivocations of literature.

Class struggle, that is, is displaced from the sphere of each of these practices and comes to occupy the epistemological spaces between them. Its lines are determined, not by the positions which men and women themselves actually take up and develop within each of these spheres, but by what we have already called the abstract and disembodied gladiators of 'science', 'literature' and 'ideology'. Ultimately, Althusser's work echoes not to the sound of class struggle but to the reverberating noise of empty epistemological categories clashing with one another.

Althusser has conceded the central thrust of this criticism.[6] Rather than regarding science and ideology as the equivalent of the fixed poles truth and falsehood, his more recent position is that a conception exists and can be identified as ideological only in the respect that it departs from the 'knowledge' proposed by a particular science. Adopting Spinoza's maxim of *verum index sui et falsi* – a science is the measure both of its own truth value and of what is false in relation to it – Althusser thus represents ideology as consisting of those ideas which *any* science regards as false in relation to its own claims to knowledge.

The difficulty is that, although Althusser would clearly like this argument to be applied with a privileged force to Marxism, logic requires that it be applied with equal force to *any* science or, indeed, any system of thought which claims to be a science. Given this, any system of ideas, including the so-called 'sciences', may appear as ideological or non-ideological according to the vantage point from which it is viewed. If the term 'ideology' is to imply, in some sense, 'that which is not true' then it can only be consistently and meaningfully used in relation to some stated criteria of veracity. However, as these vary from one theoretical context to another – the standards which obtain in Marxism, for example, are not the same as those which obtain in non-Marxist sociology – it follows that there can be no such 'thing' as ideology. There are and can be no ideas, no signifying practices which are inherently ideological in the sense that they are distortions of the 'truth' or 'misrecognitions' of 'reality'. There can only be a series of relative propositions to the effect that proposition 'x' appears to be ideological – that is, not true – when viewed from theoretical position 'y'.

Yet the very meaning of the concept of 'literature' which Althusser had earlier proposed depended entirely on its position as a kind of epistemological mediator between science and ideology. Its distinctive 'aesthetic effect' is specifically installed mid-way between the 'know-ledge effect' of science and the effect of 'misrecognition' of ideology. The effect of calling these categories into question is thus necessarily to question the validity of the concept of 'literature' if this is taken to refer to a distinct form of cognition. Lacking any anchorage in a fixed epistemological distinction between science and ideology, it simply collapses as a category.

More important, perhaps, these difficulties bring into focus the sheer incoherence of maintaining that 'literature' was installed mid-way between 'science' and 'ideology' in the first place. For, although this sounds very fine, it is difficult to see what its meaning might be. There are three possibilities. The first is that literature is installed mid-way between science in general and ideology in general. But this will not do because, as we have seen, there are no such things. The distinction between science and ideology can only be drawn within a particular science as a line dividing those statements which conform to the canons of scientificity proposed by that science and those which do not.

A second possibility is that literature should be viewed as being installed mid-way between particular sciences and particular ideologies. Whilst this may enable some critical work to be undertaken in relation to some forms of writing – early Renaissance literature, for example, was clearly influenced by the confrontation between the developing natural sciences and the remnants of medieval ideology – there are equally vast tracts of literature in relation to which this formulation is singularly irrelevant. How could it have any bearing on the cultural practice of such 'prescientific universes' as the Homeric age?

Finally, literature could be viewed as being situated mid-way between the 'knowledge' of ideology produced by Marxism and that ideology itself. This is the formulation Althusser suggests when he argues that whereas science 'gives us' ideology in the form of a knowledge of its objective social function, literature 'gives us' that same ideology in the form of 'seeing', 'perceiving' or 'feeling'. All well and good. I have no objections to such a formulation provided that its real nature is fully understood. For, in speaking of 'literature' in this way, we are in no sense speaking of a fixed body of texts which, naturally and spontaneously, exists in some objective, socially available space between science and ideology as equally natural and pre-given forms of cognition. It is rather *Marxist criticism itself* which does the placing.

Brecht's work, for example, is not in any sense 'placed' mid-way between Marxism and ideology. Nor, to take some of Eagleton's more particular formulations, can the work of Dickens or George Eliot be viewed as being 'placed' mid-way between the dominant ideological forms of mid-nineteenth century England and a Marxist theory of the social function of those forms. But those texts *may* be so placed, by Marxist criticism, as a means for the development of its own understanding and critique of such ideological forms and their fault lines. But, in this case, what we have to deal with is a *political intervention* (masquerading as science) which so constitutes literary texts as objects of study as to transform them into the *pretexts*, the pedagogical devices, whereby the Marxist reads the chinks in the armour of dominant ideologies.

The formulation that literary texts work on and transform dominant ideological forms so as to 'reveal' or 'distance' them, then, is impossible to sustain. It is rather *Marxist criticism* which, through an active and critical intervention, so 'works' upon the texts concerned as to *make them* 'reveal' or 'distance' the dominant ideological forms to which they are *made to* 'allude'. The signification of ideology that they are thus said to have is not somehow 'natural' to them; it is not a pre-given signification which criticism passively mirrors but is a signification they are *made to have* by the operations of Marxist criticism upon them.

But this is as it should be. All forms of criticism are inescapably and necessarily active and political forms of discourse. They so work upon literary texts as to modify them. Their activities belong to those real determinants which influence and condition the life of literary texts within the real social process. This is especially true for Marxist criticism. Indeed, its *raison d'être*, it might be argued, is that it should work upon literary texts, wrenching them from the forms in which they are customarily perceived or interpreted, so as to mobilize them politically in stated directions. If so, it will perform this task all the better for doing so consciously and abandoning the masks of 'science' and 'aesthetics' which serve but to disguise its true political concerns and inhibit their development.

8

WORK IN PROGRESS

THE POST-ALTHUSSERIANS

Where does all this leave us? Where is Marxist criticism going? Where should it be going? There can be no single answer to these questions. The most that can be offered, at this stage, is a sketch of work currently in progress. Before embarking upon this, however, it may be helpful if we pause to review the central thrust of the argument so far.

Our underlying concern has been to produce a theoretical space for Marxist criticism which will be consistent with its historical and materialist premises and with its political ambitions. We have argued that, in order to clear such a space, it is necessary to beat back the undergrowth of bourgeois aesthetic theory with which, for a variety of historical reasons, Marxist criticism has become entangled. We have sought, by considering Althusser's work, to show why this is so. Further, by reviewing the work of the Russian Formalists, we have sought to identify some of the concepts and analytical tools which seem to suggest the means whereby a genuinely historical and materialist study of literary texts might be inaugurated.

It is worth singling out two or three points for particular mention. First, on the question of the production of literary texts, we have tried to show how the idealist categories which Althusser derives from bourgeois aesthetics and epistemology inhibit the realization of his materialist ambitions. His approach to literary texts is quite decidedly 'formalist' in the more general and pejorative sense of that word. It is, moreover, difficult to see any respects in which his position is an advance on the particular variant of 'formalism' proposed by the Russian Formalists. The formulation that literature 'gives us' ideology in the form of 'seeing' in contradistinction to the conceptual knowledge of ideology provided by Marxist science remains, in many respects, identical with Shklovsky's proposition that literature 'creates a "vision" of the object instead of serving as a means for knowing it'.[1] All that has changed is the nature of the object – the raw material – which literary works are said to work upon and transform. For the Formalists, this raw material is provided by the structures of ordinary language and by the atrophied forms of previous literary traditions. For Althusser, by contrast, literary texts enact a process of transformation on those habituated cultural forms which, in a very special sense of the word, play an 'ideological' role within the social formation.

Given this difference, the programme mapped out for literary criticism is the same: namely, that its primary task should be to analyse the formal means whereby literary texts produce that transformation, which uniquely distinguishes them as 'literary', of the raw materials on which they work. At a technical level, the researches of the Formalists into these questions are still considerably in advance of those proposed not only by Althusser but also of those evidenced in the more detailed works of Pierre Macherey and Terry Eagleton. At this level, the work of the Althusserians remains parasitic upon that of the Formalists.

There are differences between the two positions. But these result more from Althusser's work on the concept of 'ideology' than from his particular formulations concerning 'literature'. Thus if, for Shklovsky, the work effected by the literary text promotes a renewed attentiveness to reality which is valued as an aesthetic end in itself, it is the political effect of the literary text's disruption of ideological categories that is valued by Althusser.

But herein lies the central weakness of Althusser's theory. For his theory of literature exists less in its own right than as one that is necessitated by his theory of ideology. As we have seen, he construes ideology as a universal and invariant structure which operates so as to produce in social agents forms of consciousness which will reconcile those agents to existing social relationships. Any possibility of social change demands that there be an agency – in this case, literature – which, acting in the midst of ideology, so works on it as to diminish its grip on our consciousness. Literature thus acts not merely as a mediator between ideology and science; it serves as a *necessary* agency of mediation between the two if any account is to be offered of the processes whereby the subject of an ideologically produced consciousness is to become a subject of a scientific or revolutionary consciousness.

At root, these difficulties stem from the fact that Althusser uses the term ideology to refer simultaneously, on the one hand to a particular level of social practice concerned, as we have seen, with the production of consciousness, and, on the other to a particular form of cognition which serves as the opposite of science. Given that, in this latter sense, Althusser theorizes the concept of ideology as an unchanging form of cognition within the framework of a general theory of knowledge, there was no alternative but to view literature in the same terms with, as we have seen, inescapably idealist implications.

Our first positive proposal, then, is that if we are to view literature as consisting of a set of formal operations whereby ideology is distanced and revealed, we must have in mind 'literature' as a historical and not an aesthetic category. Further, in any such formulation, we must interpret the concept of ideology politically and not epistemologically. We must, that is, use it to refer to particular forms of signification which play a particular political role in particular historical societies and not to some universal, invariant form of cognition to which there is attributed an invariant political effect. To speak of 'literature' in this way – and we have Bakhtin's work in mind – is to speak of a particular practice of writing which is moulded by a particular set of material, economic, political and ideological relationships. Only by proceeding in this way will it be possible to develop a theory of 'literature', as a sub-region of a theory of forms of fictional writing in general, which will be consistently historical and materialist in orientation.

Second, it should be recognized that any such theory of literature is a *political* one. To argue that certain forms of writing – the tradition of bourgeois *belles lettres*, say – effect a transformation of dominant ideological forms is to propose a particular *political placing* of those texts. It is to propose a particular way of looking at the relationship between different forms of cultural practice – nominated as, respectively, 'literature' and 'ideology' – which effects a particular political orchestration of those relationships. If, as Eagleton argues, the function of conventional forms of criticism is to smooth 'the troubled passage between text and reader' by soothing the contradictions within the text,[2] then a reading which aims to render that passage troublesome by *discovering* contradictions within the text is a *political intervention*. It does not restore to the text contradictions which were 'always there' but hidden from view; it *reads contradictions into the text*. It does not *reflect* a work of transformation on ideological forms that literary texts can be said always to have possessed, like some secret essence which criticism has only recently discovered; it *makes* such texts effect a work of transformation on those forms of signification which are *said to be* ideological. Put simply, there is no such spontaneous 'thing' as 'ideology' which can be said to be worked upon and transformed by an equally spontaneous 'thing' called 'literature'. There is no text which has such an 'effect' independently of the way in which it is worked by a criticism which imputes such an effect to it.

This brings us to our final point: namely, that the political effects of literary texts should be calculated in a historically concrete way. However, this involves more than merely saying that the same text should be subjected to different political calculations which reflect the different ways in which it has been appropriated during different moments of its history as a received text. It is, rather, the very nature of the object of literary criticism that is at issue.

The dominant assumption throughout the history of criticism has been that its proper object is furnished by the literary text, however 'literary' is to be defined. Within historically orientated schools of criticism, the text is construed as being, in some sense, a record of the period to which it refers. Although seemingly straightforward, this concept of the literary text as a historical record is, in fact, a double-edged one. For, apart from being regarded as a record of social customs, say, or of class-based world-views, the text is, in addition, customarily regarded as the *record of itself* – the record of its own original or true meaning, or of its own original or true political functioning or effect. It is as if, beneath the variety of historically concrete ways in which the text has been worked upon, reinterpreted, placed in different settings and so on, there is an ideal or true text which has only to be discovered for, as it were, the debate to be finally concluded.

It is this metaphysic of the text as we have called it – the concept of the text as an ideal form which has a ghostly existence behind the variant real forms in which it exists historically – that must be broken with if Marxist criticism is to be rigorously historical and materialist. Ultimately, there is no such thing as 'the text'. There is no pure text, no fixed and final form of the text which conceals a hidden truth which has but to be penetrated for criticism to retire, its task completed. There is no once-and-for-all, final truth about the text which criticism is forever in the process of acquiring. The text always and only exists in a variety of historically concrete forms. It always and only exists in the midst of those concrete and changing real determinants – such as typographical and ideological determinants, its mode of social use, the institutional setting and so on – which condition the concrete and changing ways in which it is appropriated during its history. Beyond these particular and differing texts, or, as the Formalists would have put it, particular and differing *functions* of the text, there is no such thing as a pure or limiting text except in a notional sense. It is in this deep and radical way that each age, by producing its own texts, produces its own literature.

These, then, are the three points that we are anxious to drive home. First, that a historical and materialist theory of the production of different forms of writing demands a prior break with the concerns of bourgeois aesthetics. Second, that the concept of the *text* must be replaced by the concept of the concrete and varying, historically specific *functions* and *effects* which accrue to 'the text' as a result of the different determinations to which it is subjected during the history of its appropriation. Third, that any enterprise in criticism is essentially a political undertaking. Criticism is not a 'science' which has in view, as its goal, a day when its knowledge of the pre-given universe of literary texts will be complete. It is an active and ongoing part of the political process, defined by a series of interventions within, and struggles for, the uses to which so-called literary texts are to be put within the real social process.

Most of these positions are discernible, in a more or less developed form, in the work of the 'post-Althusserians' – that is, of those critics who, deriving their broad theoretical inspiration from Althusser, would accept many of the criticisms made earlier and, much as was the case with the relationship between Bakhtin and the Russian Formalists, have been engaged in a process of *working through* Althusser to produce a new set of concerns which goes *beyond* those embodied in his work.

MODES OF LITERARY PRODUCTION

Terry Eagleton's *Criticism and Ideology* has been hailed as 'the first major study in Marxist literary theory to be written in England in forty years'.[3] Yet, for all that, it is an uneasy book, riddled by a series of significant tensions between idealist and materialist principles of analysis. On the one hand, in defining 'literature' as a form of cognition which stands mid-way between 'the distancing rigour of scientific knowledge and the vivid but loose contingencies of the "lived" itself',[4] Eagleton would seem to take on board all of the epistemological paraphernalia of Althusser's theory of literature. The difficulty is that, although this *seems* to be the case, Eagleton's more detailed considerations of the tradition running from Dickens to Joyce in fact suggest a different approach to literature as a form of signifying practice which operates at the *points of contradiction between competing ideologies*. Yet Eagleton is unable fully to articulate this quite different formulation precisely because of the epistemological baggage which he, by and large, simply takes on trust from Althusser. On the other hand, whilst proposing a detailed system of concepts which will enable literary production to be explained in materialist terms, Eagleton is unable to use these concepts precisely because he has already defined literature in idealist terms. The result is a curious game of hide-and-seek in which a new concept of literature as a particular, historically determined form of writing and a new set of concepts by means of which its particularity might be explained constantly evade one another.

So far as literary production is concerned, Eagleton proposes a system of concepts which translate, into the terms appropriate to literature, Althusser's contention that any social practice is to be understood as a process of transformation of a determinate raw material into a determinate product through the use of determinate means of production within the context of determinate social relations of production. He thus argues that literary practice is to be understood as a process of production effecting a transformation of the raw material furnished by (a) the literary traditions, genres and conventions constituted by the available 'aesthetic ideology', and (b) the discourses, values and beliefs which constitute the dominant forms of 'general ideology'. This process of transformation is enacted with the instruments of literary production furnished by the techniques and devices available to the writer within the given region of 'aesthetic ideology'. Finally, this whole process of transformation operates within the context of particular 'literary modes of production'. By 'literary modes of production', Eagleton has in mind the variety of the different social forms in which the production, exchange and reading of literature have been organized and carried out, from patronage systems of various sorts to the contemporary organization of literary production on a market basis.

It is clear that the key concept in all of this is that of 'literary mode of production' by which Eagleton signals that the literary text is to be referred back to and understood in the context of those material and social relationships which most immediately fashion its making. Paradoxically, this is a ground that has been little occupied by Marxist criticism and it is to sociology that we must look for the most fully developed exploration of these matters. Unfortunately, sociologists have broached the study of, for example, patronage systems or the organization of the literary market largely in a positivist spirit. Whilst there exists a good deal of information on these matters, they are only too often posited as a series of external 'facts' which do not connect with the literary text so as to illuminate the principles of its organization. Eagleton makes it clear that this is not the approach he has in mind:

> We are not merely concerned with the sociological outworks of the text; we are concerned rather with how the text comes to be what it is because of the specific determinations of its mode of production. If LMP's (literary modes of production) are historically extrinsic to particular texts, they are equally internal to them: the literary text bears the impress of its historical mode of production as surely as any product secretes in its form and materials the fashion of its making.[5]

The literary text is to be read, then, so as to reveal, within its formal organization, the impress of the conditions of its own making. The only difficulty is that, in spite of the centrality he accords the concept of 'literary mode of production' and the claims he makes on its behalf, Eagleton never actually *uses* it.

The reason for this can be reduced to Eagleton's constant equivocation between two different objects of study which he never clearly disentangles. At one level, in speaking of 'literary modes of production' and the other forces structuring literary practice, Eagleton clearly has in mind the generic category of 'literature' as referring to all forms of imaginative writing. Indeed, he interprets the concept even more broadly in referring, several times, to 'oral' or 'preliterate' literary modes of production. At another level, however, Eagleton's concern is with 'literature' in the more specific sense of a particular form of writing characterized by the distancing operations to which it subjects the received categories of dominant ideological forms.

Much confusion might have been avoided if, instead of speaking of 'literary modes of production', Eagleton had spoken of 'modes of cultural production', reserving the concept of 'mode of literary production' for those specific relationships of cultural production which support 'literature' as a more limited, historically specific form of writing.

Eagleton seems constantly to hover before this step without ever actually taking it. For he clearly recognizes that there may be certain 'literary modes of production' which, in subordinating literary producers to the dominant ideological apparatuses, give rise to forms of writing in which the relationship between literary text and dominant ideology is one of identity. It is thus that he refers to the tribal bard as a 'professional ideologue of the social formation' and to the medieval author as 'typically a cleric, part of an ideological apparatus'.[6] This implication is reinforced by the great play which is made of the *uniqueness* of the capitalist literary mode of production – the position of the literary producer in the market place – in securing a certain degree of independence for the writer from dominant ideological apparatuses.

It would therefore seem reasonable to regard those forms of writing which *do* distance dominant ideological categories as the product of particular relations of cultural production. For in his actual handling of the concept of 'literature' as opposed to his formal statements of definition, Eagleton moves away from Althusser in arguing that literature is determined not so much by its position of mediation between science and ideology as epistemological categories as by its location at the point of intersection of competing ideologies.

This comes across most forcibly in Eagleton's comments on the problem of literary value. These are curious in themselves. On the one hand, Eagleton argues that there is no such thing as intrinsic value:

> For there is no 'immanent' value – no value which is not *transitive*. Literary value is a phenomenon which is *produced* in that ideological appropriation of the text, that 'consumptional production' of the work, which is the act of reading. It is always *relational* value: 'exchange-value'.[7]

Yet, on the other hand – and he will brook no argument – the works of the 'great tradition' *are* indisputably of aesthetic value. And the reason for this is not because they rise above the conditions of their making but, to the contrary, because the conditions of their making are inscribed within their structure. Quixotic in the extreme, Eagleton avoids fetishizing literary value as an immanent quality of the text only to present it as an effect of the work's origins.

Arguing that the 'major work' is characterized by a play of signification upon signification, of form upon form, Eagleton contends that this toing and froing between different levels of discourse is produced by 'a certain curvature in the ideological space in which the text plays'.[8] This process of 'playing' reflects the operations on the dominant ideology of 'a particular dissentient conflictual position within it'.[9] Surveying the works of a series of representatives of the 'great tradition' – George Eliot, Dickens, Conrad, James, T. S. Eliot and so on – Eagleton argues that, if all of these are commonly regarded as great writers, they further have it in common (a) that their works throw into relief the 'fault lines' of bourgeois ideology, and (b) that, at the level of explanation, this was because 'by some conjuncture of elements (class, sexuality, region, nationality and so on), these writers were contradictorily inserted into an hegemonic bourgeois ideology which had passed its progressive prime . . .'[10]

Laying particular stress on the petit-bourgeois class position of the majority of these writers, Eagleton argues that it was because of their ambiguous class location that they were able to 'encompass a richer, more significant range of experience than those writers securely lodged within a single class',[11] and suggests that only writers who were so placed were 'open to the contradictions from which major literary art was produced'.[12] The conclusion he derives from this is that 'it is the production of the hegemonic formation from a particular *regressive* standpoint within it which lays the basis for literary value'.[13] It is this position, installed between ideologies, which supports the play of signification, the clash of discordant levels, that is the hallmark of the major work.

It is easy to see how several different sets of problems are confused here. As an attempt to deal with the problem of literary value, Eagleton's theory must be judged a failure. For there is simply no way in which a given text can be said to be valued *because of* the circumstances of its production. At root, Eagleton realizes this, and his comments on the problem of literary value become successively more contorted as he attempts to reconcile this realization with the conviction that there is something specific about the works which comprise the 'great tradition' which he does not wish to surrender to those forms of populism which would claim the parity or equivalence of all forms of writing.

We agree. But the way to theorize this specificity is historically and not aesthetically. There is, in Eagleton's comments on the problem of literary value, a real potential for the construction of a materialist concept of 'literature'. All that is necessary is to conceive the play of form upon form not as a distinguishing feature of 'major works' but as a characteristic mark of bourgeois *belles lettres* as a particular historical form of writing, leaving aside the question of the production of those texts as *valued* texts as a completely separate problem. Once this is done, the way is clear to an investigation of the particular constellation of linguistic, ideological and economic determinants which bear upon such a form of writing so as to produce for it that space, installed between ideologies, which defines it. After all, not all ideologies are spontaneously in a condition of crisis. To the contrary, they are thrown into crisis only by the nay-saying power of the ideologies which face them, and it is far from being the case, historically speaking, that all dominant ideologies have been faced with developed counter-ideologies: certainly not to the extent that they have influenced the major forms of writing. As Eagleton admits, 'ideologies without litera-ture have certainly existed'.[14] If so, this naturally raises the question as to the nature of the necessary material pre-conditions which must be satisfied for the emergence of those forms of writing which do distance ideological forms.

If Eagleton does not address this problem, it is because he has an answer ready to hand. 'Literature' is pre-defined as an abstract and eternal aesthetic category which, resurrecting the terms of a familiar idealism, Eagleton 'explains' as a part of the self-activity of ideology which is itself viewed, in a final reification, as the subject of its own process. There are thus several instances in which Eagleton suggests that ideology is to be viewed as the subject which governs the literary process through which it itself is distanced or thrown into relief. 'We are concerned', he writes, 'with the specific operations whereby the ideological produces within itself that internal distanciation which is the aesthetic.'[15] It is true that Eagleton is aware of the dangers he runs here. And he has stated earlier:

> One might even risk saying that the text is the process whereby ideol-ogy enters into a mode of relation with itself peculiarly enabling of its self-reproduction. Such a formulation can easily be misunderstood in Hegelian terms – the text as a point where the spirit of ideology enters upon a material incarnation only to reappropriate itself, literature as a mere passage or transaction within ideology itself. It is to avoid such a misconception that we need to speak of a relation of production between text and ideology.[16]

Nevertheless, such misconceptions are justified so long as the analy-sis of the process whereby the literary text works on ideology remains ungrounded in an analysis of those relations of literary production which permit the very existence of the 'literary' as a distinct sphere of operations on the 'ideological'.

LITERATURE AND THE SOCIAL PROCESS

We come, finally, to consider once again the work of Pierre Macherey whose *A Theory of Literary Production* is, in many senses, the classic text of the tradition. Clearly the inspiration behind Althusser's particular formulations of the concept of literature, it is also the acknowledged source for Terry Eagleton's work.[17] However, although proposing a far more subtle and flexible set of relationships between literature and ideology than Althusser's somewhat programmatic pronouncements on these matters, this early work nevertheless reflected Althusser's more general concerns in its attempt to situate literature mid-way between science and ideology as part of a tripartite set of epistemological distinctions.

It is all the more interesting, therefore, that it should be Macherey who has spearheaded the call for a break with aesthetics. Disputing 'the illusion that literature in general exists', Macherey, as we have seen, has more recently contended that there is no sense to the question 'What is literature?' or, rather, that such sense as it does possess derives from its presupposition that 'literature is something, that is to say a whole united around a coherent system of principles which ensure its conformity to a fixed and immutable essence'.[18] To the contrary:

> *Literature is a practical, material process of transformation* which means that in particular historical periods, literature exists in different forms. What needs to be studied is the difference between these forms. Literature with a capital 'L' does not exist; there is the 'literary', literature or literary phenomena within social reality and this is what must be studied and understood.[19]

He furthermore contends, in co-authorship with Étienne Balibar, that the question of the relationship between literature and ideology must be posed in terms which escape the 'confrontation of universal essences in which many Marxist discussions have found themselves enclosed'.[20] In speaking of 'literature', Macherey and Balibar make it unequivocally clear that they have in mind solely the condition of literary texts within bourgeois society. They contend that both the production of these texts as particular forms of the practice of writing and the determinate way in which they are currently produced for consumption or used within the social process 'require the material conditions unique to the bourgeois social formation, and are transformed with it'.[21]

More radically, Macherey breaks unequivocally with what we have called 'the metaphysic of the text'. Urging that the concept of the 'text' or the 'work' that has for so long been the mainstay of criticism should be abandoned, he advances the argument we have noted above: that there are no such 'things' as works or texts which exist independently of the functions which they serve or the uses to which they are put and that these latter should constitute the focal point of analysis. The text must be studied not as an abstraction but in the light of the determinations which, in the course of its history, successively rework that text, producing for it different and historically concrete effects in modifying the conditions of its reception.

These theoretical shifts reflect, in the main, the influence of the work of Renée Balibar and Dominique Laporte on the functioning of literary texts within the French educational system in the nineteenth century. During the Ancien Régime, it is argued, the split between 'literature' and 'non-literature' was a split between writing and non-writing, between reading and non-reading. In a society of limited literacy characterized by a split between the official language of the court and the spoken language of the people, 'literary' texts – meaning, in this case, philosophical, theological and historical as well as fictional forms of writing – symbolized and perpetuated class divisions at the level of language simply by virtue of being written and as a result of the language in which they were written. The central question to which Balibar and her co-workers have addressed themselves in the two studies they have so far produced – *Les Français Fictifs* and *Le Français National* – concerns the processes whereby 'certain writings (or readings?) are singled out, valorized, and recognized as literary in modern society where literature is no longer a question of a social category openly denoting a privileged access to reading and writing'.[22]

They have sought to answer this question by considering the social function served by the production of certain forms of fictional writing as 'literature' – that is, as a special and privileged form of writing – in nineteenth-century France. Basically, their thesis is that, in the context of the development of a uniform national language, the production of certain texts as 'literary' in this sense together with their restricted use within the education system was a manifestation of class struggle in the sphere of language: a tactic by which the bourgeoisie created and reproduced for itself a position of supremacy in language.

The argument is a complex one and we can only attempt the briefest of summaries here. Its main thrust is that the displacement of regional and class dialects and idioms by a uniform French language was, politically and ideologically speaking, a double-edged process. On the one hand, it constituted a necessary precondition for the formation of capitalism in the respect that it was necessary to effect the free circulation of commodities on a national scale. It was further necessary in that it alone could provide the necessary linguistic basis for the juridical preconditions for the development of the wage-labour relationship based on the principle of legal contracts between the seller of labour-power (the worker) and its purchaser (the capitalist). Only the formation of a common language permitted the development of a legal system based on contracts formed between ostensibly equal subjects who occupy a free and equal relation to one another within language. Finally, it constituted the necessary precondition for the emergence of republican political institutions in enabling all citizens to take part directly in public affairs without interpreters.

Accordingly, both during and in the immediate aftermath of the French Revolution a distinctive ideology and politics of language was inaugurated in which local dialects were discouraged and a newly codified, uniform grammar installed as the official vehicle of communication. This process was counterbalanced, however, by the bourgeoisie's taking over and transforming the function of the élite schooling system inherited from the Ancien Régime and so preserving for itself a second, literary language by means of the privileged position accorded in that system to the study of those forms of fictional writing which were 'produced' as 'literary' texts: as superior forms of writing which 'went beyond' the simple communicative function of ordinary language. This tendency was reinforced with the development, in the second half of the nineteenth century, of a national education system split, along class lines, between its primary and secondary levels.

Within primary schools, it is argued, the sons and daughters of 'the people' received their education in the national language in the form of an administered grammar – a set of formal rules whereby the linguistic functions of subject, object, predication etc. were learned mechanically – which was derived from the grammars of the Ancien Régime. However, the generative schema of this grammar – derived from the understanding of the rules of classical languages proposed by the Ancien Régime grammarians – was, so to speak, withheld from the people. They simply received the rules and were offered no understanding of their genesis or of the logic underlying them. The study of these was reserved for the secondary schools, populated largely by the children of the bourgeoisie, and was developed chiefly through the study of comparative grammar on the basis of selected 'literary' texts.

Just as the formal, juridical equality of economic agents under capitalism turns out to be illusory given the different positions of worker and bourgeois in the relations of production, so, Balibar and Laporte argue, the apparent equality of position of French speakers in relation to the French language conceals a real, class-based inequality. The bourgeoisie, by virtue of the facility acquired from an understanding of its mechanisms, experiences that language as its own. It is at home with it, familiar with its workings. The subordinate classes, by contrast, receive that language in an administered form, handed down from above within the education system. Familiar only with its shell, they experience the language as an exclusion and a limitation in relation to the 'superior' literary language from which they are, by virtue of their class, formally excluded. It is in this sense, viewed in the light of the actual uses to which they are put in the social process, that literary texts serve as a buttress to the maintenance of bourgeois dominance in language.

It would be wrong to generalize uncritically from this study which is married fairly closely to specifically French materials. However, it is fairly clear that the uses to which literary texts have been put within the education system in Britain – uses which, from Matthew Arnold to F. R. Leavis, have evidently been concerned to reinforce a class differentiation at the level of language – suggest many parallels which are currently being explored.[23]

More interesting, from our point of view, is the methodological import of the work of Balibar and Laporte. On the question of the production of literary texts – that is, of the dominant forms of contemporary fictional writing – it is now suggested that these are 'essentially sublimations of the conflicts lived out in the practice of language'.[24] Far from seeing literary practice as an activity which makes visible the operations of dominant ideology in any transparent sense, it is now argued that literary practice constitutes an essentially ideological operation in its attempts to heal or placate class and ideological contradictions inscribed within language itself.

Installed on a contradiction within language, the literary text is structured by an interplay between the level of ordinary grammar and that of its own distinctively literary language. The work it effects – although never with complete success – is such as to overlay or soothe these contradictions, to preserve the fiction of 'one language'. The literary text does not have an 'aesthetic effect' which is opposed to that of dominant ideology. It acts rather as a privileged region of ideology within which, by concealing its contradictions as they manifest themselves at the level of language, the whole system of dominant ideology is reproduced, preserved intact as an ongoing system in spite of the tensions with which it is racked. And criticism, far from producing a knowledge of the ideology-distancing mechanisms of literature, must set out 'to read the ideological contradictions within the devices produced to conceal them, to reconstitute the contradictions from the system of their concealment'.[25]

It is, however, in Renée Balibar's approach to the 'consumptional production' of literary texts – to the varying uses to which they are put – that the decisive theoretical break is finally located. Breaking completely with 'the metaphysic of the text', she suggests a way in which the question of the varying functions fulfilled by the text may be analysed concretely and theorized historically in the light of the concrete determinations which bear on the uses to which the text is put within the social process. The analysis she offers of two contrasting uses to which two texts, both bearing the signature of 'George Sand', have been put will serve to make the point.

The first concerns the use of an edited passage from Sand's *The Devil's Pool* which formed the basis for a series of grammatical exercises in an elementary language primer dated 1914:

(Exercise no.) 318. Copy out the following passage, putting the *subjects* in brackets.

Ploughing scene

The day was clear and mild, and the soil, freshly cleft by the plough-share, sent up a light steam. At the other extremity of the field, an old man was gravely driving his plough of antique shape, drawn by two placid oxen, true patriarchs of the meadow, tall and rather thin, with pale yellow coats and long drooping horns. They were those old workers who, through long habit, have grown to be brothers. The old labourer worked slowly, silently, and without waste of effort. His docile team were in no greater haste than he; but, thanks to the undistracted steadiness of his toil, his furrow was soon ploughed.

(Exercise no.) 319. Vocabulary. 1. Give six names of agricultural implements such as *a plough*. 2. Write down six times the noun: *a field*, adding in each case a *singular* or *plural* complement, according to its meaning, e.g. a field *of wheat*, a field *of turnips*. 3. Give six feminine nouns ending in *ée* like *la journée*.[26]

Here, then, we have, in a particular determinate form, a text bearing the signature 'George Sand' which can be said to have 'effects' only through the use to which it is put. In this case, in the context of elementary schooling, the work is used for teaching the abstracted functions of grammar. The pupil is to abstract from their particular exemplars contained in the text the grammatical functions of nouns, the concepts of singular, plural, etc. The text functions to teach rules that must be complied with, not understood.

That is the 'national language' in one form. Let us now see 'the same' passage as it appears in a 1962 'critical edition' of George Sand's works, specially prepared for use in secondary and higher education:

At the other extremity of the field, an old man, whose broad shoulders and stern face recalled Holbein's ploughman, but whose clothes car-ried no suggestion of poverty, was gravely driving his swing-plough of antique shape drawn by two placid oxen, true patriarchs of the meadow, tall and rather thin, with pale, yellow coats and long droop-ing horns. They were those old workers who, through long habit, have grown to be brothers, as they are called in our country, and who, when one loses the other, refuse to work with a new comrade, and pine away with grief. People who are unfamiliar with the country call the love of the ox for his yoke-fellow a fable. Let them come and see in the corner of the stable one of these poor beasts, thin and wasted, restlessly lashing his lean flanks with his tail, violently breathing with mingled terror and disdain on the food offered him, his eyes always turned towards the door, scratching with his hoof the empty place at his side, sniffing the yokes and chains which his fellow used to wear, and incessantly calling him with melancholy lowings . . .

The old labourer worked slowly, silently, and without waste of effort. His docile team were in no greater haste than he; but, thanks to the undistracted steadiness of his toil and the judicious expenditure of his strength, his furrow was as soon ploughed as that of his son, who was driving, at some distance from him, four less vigorous oxen through a more stubborn and stony piece of ground.[27]

Here we have 'the same' text, in a different form, fulfilling different functions and giving rise to different effects. The entire grammatical structure of the passage has been altered by the different use of punctuation, replacing the simple sentence structure of subject-verb-predicate by a more complex structure in which subordinate clauses, phrases in apposition etc. proliferate. The *words* are, for the greater part, the same; but the *language* is different. The complexities which characterize the second passage have been flattened out in the first so that simple grammatical functions might be easily identified. Moreover, the allusions of the two passages are different. The allusions of the first passage are technical; ploughing is described as a simple agricultural process. Those in the second are pastoral and cultural: rural life is aestheticized and, at the same time, constant allusions are made to the stock cultural themes of the bourgeois humanist tradition. There is the reference to Holbein reinforced, Balibar tells us, by an engraving by Holbein which appears in an earlier chapter of the 'critical edition' and, at various points in the editors' annotations, references to Albrecht Dürer, Michelangelo, Goya and so on.

One could go on. But the point is that here we have two passages, bearing a signature authenticating them as the product of the same author. Nevertheless, placed in different contexts (primary as against secondary or higher education) and 'produced' by different determinants (grammatical exercises as opposed to the cultural references which surround the text in the 'critical edition'), these two passages, although ostensibly the same, fulfil different functions and give rise to different effects. *Neither one of these is the 'original' or 'true' text. Nor is either of them the bastardized version of the other. They are, simply, different texts.* And there is no pure or limiting text – there is no 'real' or 'essential' George Sand – which might be invoked to adjudicate between them except on grounds of scholarly accuracy. There was, that is to say, a first date of publication for *The Devil's Pool* (1846) and, in this sense, an 'original' form of the text (it appeared in serial form in a liberal newspaper). Whilst this must serve as the critical standard against which the accuracy of subsequent editions must be checked, the *particular form* of this text, the moment of its appearance and the intervention it embodied, is in no sense *ontologically privileged* in relation to subsequent forms of the text as, for example, in the critical edition cited. Both are equally real; both have given rise to real effects; both need analysis in their specificity.

The text is always 'worked'. In one form or another, in the variant forms of its concrete existence, it always comes to us overlayered by the different determinants – the uses to which it is put, the annotations which are appended to it, the editor's preface, the design of the cover – which 'produce' it for consumption in a concrete form. It is here, and nowhere else, that the effects of the text must be analysed.

However, this is not merely an advance of methodological significance. It is also a *political* advance. 'The philosophers,' Marx wrote, 'have only *interpreted* the world, in various ways; the point is to change it.'[28] Marxist critics, it might similarly be argued, have merely interpreted literature in various ways. The point is to change it, to so work upon those determinations which condition the real social functioning of the literary text as to change the uses to which it is put. Renée Balibar's work maps out not merely a new field for criticism; it maps out a new field for practice.

Exactly how this new field for practice should be viewed and how Marxists should enter it are questions that can only be briefly commented upon here. At root, however, both have to do with the positions that different cultural forms and practices occupy in relation to one another within the internal disposition of a given 'cultural field'. By 'cultural field' or 'field of cultural relationships', I mean simply to refer to the set of structural relationships which fix and define the position of different forms of cultural practice with reference to one another and which, in so doing, produce for them their role and function, their effectivity, within the social process.

It follows from all that has been maintained so far that the position of any form of cultural practice within this field is never fixed for all time. Just as there is no permanent line of demarcation between the 'literary' and the 'non-literary', so there is no once-and-for-all boundary that can be drawn between dominant and oppositional cultural practices. The position of a given form of cultural practice within the disposition of a given cultural field and, accordingly, the part it plays within the wider social process are constantly shifting and changing as the relationships which define that field are themselves constantly redefined and rearticulated. There are no forms of cultural practice which are intrinsically and forever either dominant or oppositional. Their functioning and effect, in political terms, depend on the place they occupy within that incessantly changing nexus of relationships which defines their position in relation to one another.

The practice of literary criticism, it has been argued, has played an important role in structuring the field of cultural relations in a certain way, producing for so-called 'literary' texts a particular position within that field as the supports for the maintenance of bourgeois hegemony at the level of language. This position, it is important to stress, is in no sense natural to such texts. It is a product of a historically particular organization of the field of cultural relations and of the particular way in which the texts concerned are produced for consumption within that field. It can therefore be changed. In effecting a redefinition of the cultural field, in shifting the ways in which the relationships between the various forms of cultural practice which comprise it are viewed, Marxist criticism may contribute to such a change.

The politics of literature, on this construction, are inseparable from the politics of criticism. Marxist criticism has hitherto proceeded on the assumption that every literary text has its politics inscribed within it and that the role of Marxist criticism is to enunciate this politics, to give it voice by making it explicit. This political essentialism must be broken with. The text does not have a politics which is separable from the determinations which work upon it or the position it occupies within the disposition of the field of cultural relations. The task which faces Marxist criticism is not that of reflecting or of bringing to light the politics which is already there, as a latent presence within the text which has but to be made manifest. It is that of *actively politicizing* the text, of *making its politics for it*, by producing a new position for it within the field of cultural relations and, thereby, new forms of use and effectivity within the broader social process.

9

CONCLUSION

Literary criticism, as we know it, has well over a century of accredited activity behind it. It has developed a language which absolutely saturates the field and holds powerful and entrenched positions within the bastions of academia. Through their grip on examination boards and their control over the training of teachers, the literature departments of our universities effectively determine both *what* literature should be taught and *how* it should be taught – what questions should be put to it – throughout the entire context of secondary and tertiary education. In this way, the discourses of literary criticism developed at the frontiers of academic life reach back, through a variety of well-worn institutional paths, to condition the ways in which literary texts are used within those ideological processes by which we, millions of us, make sense, or have sense made for us, of our lives.

Viewed in this light, literary criticism is not an expensive luxury. To the contrary, as what has proved to be the most potent vehicle for the peddling of all sorts of ideological wares and mythologies, it is money well spent. The uses to which literary texts are put within the social process constitute the most privileged mode of reproduction and social relay of the bourgeois myths which disperse men and women, along with their history, into a frozen world of idealist and essentialist categories. Myths of creation, of genius, of man's essential nature, of the eternality and universality of the forms by which we express ourselves are all strongly supported in this way.

Apart from the odd left-wing literary mole burrowing away from within, the institutional power of orthodox literary criticism remains substantially unchallenged. Yet, at the theoretical level, its grip has been noticeably weakened. A revolution in thought first presents itself in the guise of a questioning or reformulation of old problems and the production of new ones. Until recently, Marxist critics have failed to meet this challenge. They competed with bourgeois criticism, but did not displace it. The significance of the new directions in Marxist criticism we have surveyed in this study is that they push the critical edge of Marxism one step further. They question not merely the answers but the questions, the founding assumptions of bourgeois criticism and propose, in their place, a quite new, radically different set of concerns.

Yet, although it has been contended that the central question of bourgeois criticism – 'What is Literature?' – is a misplaced one, it has proved to be easier to denounce this question than to jettison it completely. For it is easier to announce a 'theoretical break' than to complete it. Revolutions in thought do not occur overnight. They are difficult and protracted processes hindered at every step by the weight of received concepts which, lingering on, influence the thought of even those who lead the call to break with them. We have thus shown how, in the work of Althusser and Eagleton, the question 'What is Literature?', although absent in the sense that it is never explicitly put, is effectively present in the answers it elicits. Althusser and Eagleton do not ask the question 'What is Literature?' But they answer it.

The stress on capitals – on Literature – is important here. For one must take care not to throw the baby out with the bath water. Beneath the concern with the specificity of Literature as a privileged and specializing category, there remains a further problem. For if one admits that the concept of Literature is a false abstraction from the sphere of fictional writing in general, the problem of the distinction between fictional writing as a general category and nonfictional discourses – such as those of science or philosophy – remains.

This is not, it must be stressed, the problem of 'What is Literature?' in another guise. Any theory of writing must address both the similarities and the differences between forms of writing. The crucial differences between such theories therefore relate to how they articulate the relationship between such relations of difference and similarity. Within traditional aesthetics, these problems are entered, through the pre-emptive enclosure of Literature as a hermetically separate enclave of cultural practice. The differences that are to be explained are, first, those between Literature and non-fictional discourses and, second, those between Literature and other, 'degraded' forms of fictional writing. The similarities to be examined are those within the sphere of Literature itself. A possible third question – 'What do all forms of fictional writing have in common?' – is either suppressed or simply neglected. What is thus offered is usually a twofold set of distinctions. First, Literature is distinguished, exclusively on the basis of the 'great works', from non-fictional discourses; second, the separation of this category of works from all other forms of fictional writing is justified in terms of valuational criteria – depth of feeling, universality of senti-ment, etc. – which, as the case may be, may or may not have any connection with the first axis of differentiation. The result is that those forms of fictional writing which do not fall within the category of Literature are considered only negatively as the pale, inferior imitations of the privileged category of works from which they are excluded. They exist only to be condemned.

The procedural implications of Macherey's more recent concern with the problem of the 'fiction effect' are entirely the reverse of this. They are that one should first establish the similarities between differ-ent forms of fictional writing and then go on to examine the differ-ences between them. This not only forestalls the ritual, more or less obligatory condemnation of fictional forms which fall outside the received tradition. It also, provided that one foregoes the temptation to reintroduce the concept of Literature through the back door, enables one to explain the differences between different types of fiction in materialist terms.

Yet the temptation is a strong one. The privileged concept of Litera-ture survives, quite transparently in the case of Althusser, in the formu-lation that Literature – only 'genuine literature', that is – effects a certain productive transformation of ideology which offers its work-ings to view. If this is true only of major forms of writing, the question naturally arises: What about the others? What do they do? Althusser has no answer whereas Eagleton recognizes the problem only to sidestep it, to transform it into the problem of value. There are, he affirms, forms of writing which do not operate upon ideology in the way outlined but which, instead, move within the withered ideological matrices of received myths without in any sense rupturing them. And that, he suggests, is why they are inferior. The condemnation is reflex. Such works are inferior because they are not great, and they are not great because their conditions of production are not the same as those which underlie and produce great works.

This is not to say that some forms of writing should not be condemned and others preferred. But it is *we* who do the condemning; *we* who do the preferring, and on grounds that have to be argued and struggled for. There neither is nor can be a science of value. Value is something that must be produced. A work is of value only if it is valued, and it can be valued only in relation to some particular set of valuational criteria, be they moral, political or aesthetic. The problem of value is the problem of the social production of value; it refers to the ever ongoing process whereby which texts are to be valued and on what grounds are incessantly matters for debate and, indeed, struggle. Value is not something which the text has or possesses. It is not an attribute of the text; it is rather something that is produced for the text. To neglect this, to reify the text as the source of its own value, is to run together two quite distinct problems: the explanation of the text as the product of a particular practice of writing and the production of a text as a valued text. The result, as in Eagleton's suggestion that a text's value somehow derives from the conditions of its production, and, thereafter, clings to it through subsequent conditions of the text's existence, is that the task of explaining the text is given a particular, pre-emptive skew in the respect that any such explanation must simultaneously present itself as an explanation of the text's value.

Macherey's concern with the 'fiction effect' avoids this pre-emptive closure of the way in which Marxists should concern themselves with the history of writing. Although insisting on a necessary separation between the literary (as a general category) and the ideological, and construing the literary as a distinctive sphere of operations on the ideological which gives rise to a distinctive 'fiction effect', Macherey's approach allows the study of the history of writing to be conducted much more open-endedly. It is not Literature that effects a certain productive transformation of ideology, but literature – that is, all forms of fictional writing. The concern, within such an approach, is with the different sets of formal devices through which different forms of writing work upon ideology so as to produce it in different ways – sometimes distancing it, sometimes underwriting its effects by sealing its enclosures. To plagiarize Eagleton's key concept, the concern of Marxist criticism should be with the differences between different literary modes of the production or transformation of ideology. Not a theory of Literature, but a theory of literatures: concrete, historically specific and materialistic.

There is a second set of problems which, although related to the above, should not be confused with it: the production of 'Literature', that is, the social production of texts as Literary and of the effects which thus accrue to them in the light of the position which they occupy in relation to other texts and the uses to which they are put within the social process. In spite of all its apparent concreteness and facticity, the text is not the place where the business of culture is conducted. Culture is not a thing but a process and a system of relationships within which the production of meaning takes place. Within that process, the rituals and artefacts which constitute the visible surface of culture – books, paintings, rituals of consumption – are constantly rearticulated in relation to one another. The self-same objects and practices are constantly placed within different contexts and put to different uses as the relationships between them are constantly reshuffled. This is easily observed in the case of the visual arts where images are often physically transported from one location (churches) to another (art-galleries) and, in the process, used as the basis for the production of different meanings. But the same is true of written texts. The text is not the issuing source of meaning. It is a site on which the production of meaning – of variable meanings – takes place. The social process of culture takes place not within texts but between texts, and between texts and readers: not some ideal, disembodied reader, but historically concrete readers whose act of reading is conditioned, in part by the text it is true, but also by the whole ensemble of ideological relationships which bear upon the incessant production and reproduction of texts.

The world of appearances, in the arena of literary criticism, is doubly deceptive. The apparently concrete, the text, turns out, on further inspection, to be an abstraction whereas the apparently abstract, the system of relationships between texts, proves to be the concrete or, more accurately, a necessary abstraction through which it is alone possible to encounter the text in its particular, determinate and historically varying concrete forms. The concrete, Marx remarks in the *Grundrisse*, is the result and not the point of departure for thought. The concrete is the concrete, he argues, only because it is the concentration of many determinations whose interaction, far from being given spontaneously to view, can only be grasped through the violent abstraction of thought. One reaches the concrete only via a detour. So long as criticism refuses that detour and remains ensnared within the false concrete of the immediately given – the text – the truly concrete will elude it.

AFTERWORD

I am struck, looking back over the twenty-five years since the first publication of *Formalism and Marxism*, by four really quite decisive changes in the intellectual contexts bearing upon its central preoccupations. The first concerns what has proved to be, especially since 1989, the quite unstoppable decline in the influence of Marxist thought as its claims to provide a comprehensive system of historical explanation have come to look less and less persuasive. As a part and parcel of this larger picture, the declining influence of Althusserian Marxism has been particularly dramatic, partly because of the shadow cast over it by Althusser's theoretical recantations and, perhaps more tellingly, his diagnosis as insane and his confinement for murdering his wife. This has also meant, to come to the second change of context, that Althusserian literary and aesthetic theory has proved pretty much a *cul-de-sac*; certainly, while the theoretical productivity of the 'Althusserian moment' is not in question, there has, since the 1990s, been little new literary theory that has been avowedly Althusserian in its lineage or aspirations. But this has also formed part of a more general, and third, trend as questions concerning aesthetics have been significantly re-framed in the last twenty or so years as they have been translated into the broader frameworks of cultural studies – and, of late, the burgeoning field of visual culture – where they have taken on a more social and sociological slant.

A significant factor in this, to come to the fourth trend, has been the ascending influence of the work of Mikhail Bakhtin and, more generally, that of the Bakhtin school as more of this work has become available in translation and as its implications, not just for literary theory but for a much wider range of concerns, has been worked through in a now considerable and still growing literature. This last development has been especially welcome. For Bakhtin is clearly the theoretical hero of *Formalism and Marxism*, providing, in the project of a historical poetics that emerges from his work, the co-ordinating intellectual perspective that governs the book's engagements with both Russian Formalism and Althusserian aesthetic theory. At the same time, though, the Bakhtin that has emerged over the intervening period is a more complex one, far richer theoretically and with a more nuanced and ambivalent relation to Marxist thought than I had appreciated.

These, then, are the main intellectual developments that need to be reckoned with in order to resituate the concerns of *Formalism and Marxism* within the context of contemporary debates. Before I do so, however, I want to briefly review the main arguments of the book to identify the key moves it makes and their consequences. For, whatever else it might be, *Formalism and Marxism* is an argumentative study. My purpose in writing it was not to provide a disinterested account of either Russian Formalism or of Marxist literary and aesthetic theory. Rather, my aim was a more polemical one: to rub together two traditions of thought – that of the Formalists and the then emergent school of Althusserian criticism – to see what kind of critical friction might be generated as a result.

CRITICAL FRICTIONS

I can perhaps best introduce my concerns here by saying something about the circumstance that prompted the book.[1] This arose from my disagreement with Terry Hawkes and John Hartley who, in an Open University teaching unit they had written in 1976–1977, invoked Viktor Shklovsky's law of the 'canonization of the junior branch' to support their argument that there are no intrinsic differences between those forms of written fiction labelled 'popular fiction' and those labelled 'literature'.[2] I felt that this was a questionable use of Shklovsky, for two reasons. First, it did not distinguish between the two different processes to which Shklovsky's law referred. For where it refers to those processes whereby literature renews itself by drawing upon the themes, motifs and devices of 'sub-literary' genres, the distinction between 'literature' and other forms of fiction is not called into question. Popular fiction here serves merely as one among many possible sources for devices that can enable a renewal of the literary function of defamiliarization in contexts where prevailing literary conventions have become stale and atrophied. Shklovsky's law, when applied in this sense, was simply a variant of Eichenbaum's maxim that the line of literary influence runs not from father to son, but from grandfather to grandson, or from uncle to nephew, as archaic or marginal forms supply the writer with the means of displacing, estranging or subverting prevailing literary canons.

However, Shklovsky also invoked the same 'law' to refer to those processes through which specific texts, hitherto regarded as merely popular or as of a marginal significance, themselves come to occupy and fulfil the literary function of defamiliarization. Again, though, I thought this would not bear the weight that Hartley and Hawkes wanted to place on it to support the view that the textual distribution of the label 'literature' is merely a matter of taste or fashion. For Shklovsky, the process of canonization does not refer to changes in literary fashion through which the value of previously neglected texts rises within official literary canons. On the contrary, it refers to the processes through which a text previously on the margins of a literary system is able to take on the literary function of defamiliarization as a result of changes that have taken place within the organization of the inter-textual relations characterizing that system. It refers, therefore, not to the sociological determinations of literary taste, but to the changing function and significance which might accrue to particular practices of writing when the relationships which characterize the literary system in which a text is inserted are changed by new and different practices of writing or, more radically, when a text is shifted from one literary system to another.

This second usage of Shklovsky's 'law' does not dispose of the concept of literature either. But it does redefine it, and in manner that is sharply distinct from conventional views of literature as a stable corpus of texts united by shared formal attributes or a common literary essence which distinguishes them, for all time, from other forms of writing. Instead, for Shklovsky and the Russian Formalists, the concept referred to a function (defamiliarization) that could be fulfilled by different practices of writing in different literary systems, or at different points of time within the same system. The distinction is an important one in view of the potential it offers for a critique of the concept of literature that would have more far-reaching consequences than those arising from perspectives on changing literary tastes and fashions. This potential arises from the challenge the Formalists presented to the metaphysical qualities that texts assume within conventional accounts of literature. In place of the text, the Russian Formalists made the system of inter-textual relations the central object of study, viewing the meaning, functioning and significance of a given text – particularly whether, when and where it might perform the literary function of defamiliarization – as being over-determined by varying inter-textual relations, rather than guaranteed or produced solely by its intrinsic and unchanging properties.

This, then, was the theoretical 'grit' that I wanted to quarry from the Russian Formalists to use as a corrective to those tendencies within Marxist literary and aesthetic theory I wanted to question. Althusserian criticism provided a convenient route into these questions in view of the striking resemblance that was evident between its formulations and those of the Russian Formalists. For Louis Althusser, Terry Eagleton and Pierre Macherey, literature is a practice which works upon and transforms the categories of ideology in such a way as to make them visible, fore-grounding their operations by means of peculiar literary devices. This 'aesthetic effect' distinguishes literary works from the mere reproduction of ideology that is attributed to 'non-literary' (but still fictional) practices of writing, just as it is distinct from the forms of cognition afforded by science. While this echoes the Russian Formalist definition of literariness as the defamiliarization of habituated modes of cognition, there are equally important differences between the two positions, the most consequential being that neither the category of ideology nor the science/ideology couplet have any role in the writings of the Russian Formalists. That said, the theoretical logics at work in the two positions are strikingly similar. Both see literature as a transformative practice which turns habituated forms of representation and perception inside out, so to speak, thereby prompting new forms of awareness and attentiveness.

Where Althusserian criticism departs most from Russian Formalism – and largely to its disadvantage – is in its conventionalism. By putting the question of 'literariness' to one side of conventional distinctions between serious art and popular art, literature and non-literature, the Russian Formalists did not seek to rationalize or consecrate the literary canons of their period by providing them with a clear theoretical foundation. By contrast, within the writings of Eagleton and Althusser (Macherey is a more complicated case) the two problems are implicitly linked: the effect of making ideology visible produced by certain forms of textual practice is equated definitionally with the category of literature in its conventional form – that is, as a relatively fixed corpus of texts distinguished in value from other forms of writing. In this, however, they were entirely in accord with the mainstream of Marxist literary and aesthetic thought which has proved to be far less historical and materialist in practice than, in theory, it has claimed to be. A central argument of *Formalism and Marxism*, more fully elaborated in later work,[3] was that this disparity between theory and practice reflects the degree to which Marxist literary theory, by aligning its concerns with those of philosophical aesthetics, has subscribed to a set of idealist premises which have frustrated its historical and materialist ambitions at every turn. The dialogue that the book orchestrates between Formalism and Marxism is thus one which aims to turn the tables on earlier assessments of the relations between the two. On the one hand, it argues that the Russian Formalist deserve to be viewed less pejoratively than had previously been the case in Marxist circles, and that far from being focused narrowly on purely technical questions, their work raised serious and fundamental problems about conventional accounts of literature. On the other hand, it argues that Marxist criticism has been quite uncritical in its acceptance of conventional categories of literature, and that this is regrettable not merely in itself but because it has had seriously disabling consequences for the ways in which Marxists have approached a series of related critical concerns.

There are two main reasons for thinking that the problem of 'literature' and the related concerns of aesthetics sit ill at ease with Marxism's historical and materialist inclinations. First, to accept as a legitimate problem the specificity of the mode of writing embodied in a selected canon is to neglect the critical and institutional procedures which bear upon the selection and reproduction of that canon.[4] It is a problem which can be posed only by means of a systematic inattention to the ways in which certain texts are selected from the broader field of writing and produced, institutionally and discursively, as 'literature'. Second, it suggests that those texts which constitute 'literature' can be abstracted from the historically specific circumstances of their production and be grouped together precisely to the extent that they share some uniquely distinguishing set of formal properties which marks them off from other, non-literary forms of writing. This has resulted in two types of materialism: either a truncated materialism, which stops short of explicating those critically differentiating attributes which constitute the uniquely defining characteristics of 'literature' (since, by definition, these transcend their historical determination); or a one-sided materialism, which focuses on conditions of production at the expense of those conditions of consumption which produce and reproduce specific texts as valued works.

The critique of what I called 'the metaphysic of the text' – that is, the hypostatization of the text as an essentially fixed entity – that can be quarried from the work of the Formalists provides a useful counter to this second tendency. The main analytical gambit of Marxist literary theory has been to explain the specificity of literature by returning the text to the historical conditions of its production, thereby construing the text as the source of an effect – permanent and durable – which derives from its relations to those conditions of production. The history that flows into the text during the process of its production is thus privileged in being accorded an effectivity that is judged to be capable of overriding the histories that flow through the text through the diverse forms of its subsequent consumption and modes of social use. This leads to a neglect of 'the living life of the text'; that is, of the ways in which its connections with social and historical processes are changed as the relations within which reading and writing take place are subjected to constant variation.

This argument formed a part and parcel of the revised accounts of textuality arising from post-structuralism and deconstruction. However, it gave these a distinctive twist in contending that, if the properties of texts were over-determined by the systems of inter-textual relations within which they were inscribed at different historical moments, then so such systems of inter-textual relations had themselves to be understood as the product of distinctive social and ideological relations. This proved, for a time, a useful perspective,[5] albeit also a limited one which would now need to be revised in the light of the broader constellation of intellectual developments that have placed the social investigation of aesthetic forms and processes on quite new ground.

RE-FRAMING AESTHETICS

The early 1990s saw the publication of two books, each with strong affiliations to the Marxist tradition yet contrasting sharply from one another in their sense of how Marxist categories should be applied in engaging with the concerns of aesthetic theory: Terry Eagleton's *The Ideology of the Aesthetic* and Pierre Bourdieu's *The Rules of Art*. In the first of these, not a glimpse remains of the scientific formulations of Eagleton's earlier *Criticism and Ideology* where the tasks of literary theory had been expressed in almost algebraic terms: how to decipher texts as the outcomes of the relations between AI (aesthetic ideology), AuI (authorial ideology), and GI (general ideology) in the context of the place of a specific LMP (literary mode of production) within the GMP (general mode of production) prevailing at any particular historical moment.[6] What is offered, instead, is an analysis of western aesthetic theory as the site of a general contradiction in which its 'real historical complexity' is expressed. Eagleton summarizes this contradiction as follows:

> The aesthetic is at once . . . the very secret prototype of human subjectivity in early capitalist society, and a vision of human energies as radical ends in themselves which is the implacable enemy of all dominative and instrumental thought. It signifies a creative turn to the sensuous body, as well as an inscribing of that body with a subtly oppressive law; it represents on the one hand a liberatory concern with concrete particularity, and on the other hand a specious form of universalism. If it offers a generous utopian image of reconciliation

> between men and women at present divided from one another, it
> also blocks and mystifies the real political movement toward such
> historical community.[7]

A part of Eagleton's concern here is to distinguish his position on the
aesthetic as a historically distinctive mode of cognition from those of
vulgar Marxism and post-Marxism which, in an unlikely pairing, he
sees as both prone to automatically condemn a concept, practice or
institution just because their origins can be located in bourgeois society.
Concerned to provide a more historical and dialectical assessment of
the aesthetic and its contradictory legacy, what Eagleton offers, while
strong on dialectics – tracing how the contradiction summarized above
plays itself out in different ways in the writing of aesthetic theorists
from Alexander Baumgarten through to Frederic Jameson – contains
precious little by way of history. Except, that is, for history in the grand
sense. HISTORY in the upper case we might call it, in which, once
briefly evoked, the central contradictions of capitalism for each epoch
are recounted in the shadow lives that are attributed to them in the
dialectical torsions of the aesthetic texts in which they are expressed.
Such contradictions are to be worked through, but are never resolved
or considered capable of resolution until the social contradictions generating them have given way to a higher, more communal form of
social organization. This is, in short, a history of aesthetics very much
after the fashion of Georg Lukács in which big historical events constantly rumble offstage leaving the theorist free to do a little tricky
dialectical stuff without the need for any close-up investigation of the
more local and specific conditions and engagements characterizing the
actual historical circumstances in which particular aesthetic theories
and practices were produced and the distinctive forms of their social
deployment. This is necessarily so in a form of 'historical' analysis
which is constantly obliged to overlook local circumstances to see how
the same contradictions are worked out differently as they are passed
on from one aesthetic theorist to another. Its shortcomings in these
regards are only too evident when compared with the more meticulous historical excavations of, for example, Mary Poovey who – far
from seeing the aesthetic as implacably opposed to instrumental reason
– traces its early development in the work of Shaftesbury as precisely a

key instrument within the emergence of new forms of liberal government.[8]

The same is true of Bourdieu's *The Rules of Art* in view of the close attention it pays to detailed considerations concerning the organization of literary and artistic markets, their places within the cultural field, and the implications of these considerations for the calculations and strategies of different agents – writers, artists, publishers, editors, curators, gallery owners, art dealers – within the cultural field. It is here, for Bourdieu, in the more mundane calculations and actions of agents in the cultural sphere that a social account of the historical emergence of the autonomy of the aesthetic is to be found – in the production of a position of autonomy for the writer vis-à-vis economic and political power that he traces in the career of Flaubert, or in the production of the pure gaze of aesthetic contemplation whose development is coeval with that of the modern art museum. At a key point in discussing the methodological principles underlying his approach to these issues, Bourdieu compares his own approach with that of the Russian Formalists whom he viewed as being caught in a trap pretty much of their own making:

> Refusing to consider anything other than the system of works, that is, the 'network of relationships established between texts' (and secondarily, the relationships, incidentally very abstractly defined, between this network and other 'systems' functioning in the 'system-of-systems' constituting society – not so far from Talcott Parsons), these theoreticians are also forced to find in the 'literary system' itself the principle of its own dynamics.[9]

It is not, Bourdieu goes on to say, that the Formalists were unaware of the tensions between different literary schools or between the canonized and non-canonized branches of literature. Their mistake, rather, was to mistake two planes of analysis: the plane of the works in which the relations between works, or texts, are mediated via their position within the literary system, and 'the plane of objective positions in the field of production and the antagonistic interests based on them'.[10] By neglecting the latter, the Formalists were obliged to offer a single-planar analysis in which literary change emerged as a more-or-less natural law regulated by the invariant tendency of de-automatization, or defamiliarization, only to inevitably give way to a new automatization 'born of a wear-and-tear linked to a repetitive use of the means of literary expression',[11] hence generating the need for a new cycle of de-automatization. Yet Bourdieu is clear that the positive lesson he takes from the Russian Formalists is their stress on the need for analysis to deal with the properties of literary systems. Where this is not the case – and he singles out the world-view analysis of Lukács and Lucien Goldmann to make his point – the resulting forms of analysis trace too direct and reductive a connection between literary works and the values of particular social groups and classes. They thus fail to allow for the ways in which the relations of individual works to broader social processes are doubly mediated by the organization of the literary system and its place within the field of cultural production and the agents and institutions that are active there.

Bourdieu is also clear that to trace the historical genesis of the autonomy of the aesthetic to the impure conditions provided by the antagonistic interests of different agents within capitalist relations of cultural production is not, thereby, to write it off because it has its roots in bourgeois society. To the contrary, he argues that, once the autonomy of the literary and artistic fields has been established in relation to the economic and political realms, their subsequent development is governed by a cumulative logic. This process nurtures the development of those values, which Bourdieu calls the '*historical transcendental*',[12] which are critical of the fields of economic and political power. The capacity of critique is thus construed as the historical legacy of the autonomization of the aesthetic. As such, it is a capacity that can only be maintained and extended through the struggles of artists, writers and intellectuals in the cultural sphere. This is not to suggest that Bourdieu's position on these matters is without problems. What his work does represent, however, and in sharp contrast to the post-Althusserian trajectory of Eagleton's work, is an engagement with the Formalists, much like that of the Bakhtin school, that is alert to the positive qualities of their claims to scientific rigour in analysing the operations of literary systems while also overcoming their shortcomings by providing the tools of analysis that will connect those operations to broader social processes. That said, the work of Bakhtin has

also opened up other avenues of inquiry that deepen and extend the
project of a historical poetics that I flagged in *Formalism and Marxism*.

BAKHTIN AND BEYOND

I first came across the work of Bakhtin and Vološinov through
Raymond Williams – initially via his somewhat oblique reference, in
Keywords, to the 'basic work' of Vološinov alongside that of Ullmann,
Spitzer and other figures in the field of historical semantics,[13] and then
again, a year later, in the more extended discussion of Vološinov's work
in *Marxism and Literature*.[14] Williams's interests, however, concerned the
contributions of Vološinov/Bakhtin to the study of language with the
result that his focus was on the Vološinov-Vygotsky-Saussure set of
relations rather than the Russian Formalist-Bakhtin school relations
focused on questions of literature. There was, as I noted at the time,
relatively little on these questions, apart from an important essay by
Julia Kristeva, that was easily available in English translation.[15] The
situation has changed dramatically over the intervening period, with
the translation of a much greater body of writings,[16] a more authoritative state of knowledge regarding the authorship of texts bearing the
names of Bakhtin, Vološinov and Medvedev,[17] and the application of
Bakhtinian perspectives to a much broader field of debates than those
centred on questions of either language or literature.

The result, certainly, is a picture of a more complex Bakhtin, one
whose whose concerns with the interrelations of official and carnival
culture in early Renaissance literature can now be seen as part of a
much broader set of interests focused on the conditions in which
the relations between different cultures do, and do not, introduce
new forms of dynamism into the literary field. This is most evident in
The Dialogic Imagination and its account of the role of *heteroglossia* or *poly-
glossia* – the inter-animation of different cultures, languages and spatio-
temporal universes (or chronotopes) – in the development of novelistic
discourse. This clearly became his central preoccupation within the
field of historical poetics. Bakhtin did not see the novel as being, like
other genres, definable in terms of so many fixed formal properties. 'I
am not,' he wrote, 'constructing here a functional definition of the
novelistic canon in literary history, that is a definition that would make

of it a system of fixed generic characteristics'.[18] The novel's specificity consisted rather in its fluidity, reflecting an in-built capacity for change which allowed the novel to function as a dynamising force within the literary field, prompting reactive changes in other genres. Attributing this, its open-endedness and unstoppable capacity for becoming, to the novel's articulation of a multi-languaged consciousness, Bakhtin sees this as, in turn, the result of historically specific social conditions. Here is how he puts it, writing of the novel's many-languagedness, its ability to co-ordinate multiple temporal co-ordinates and its open-endedness:

> These three characteristics of the novel are all organically interrelated and have all been powerfully affected by a very specific rupture in the history of European civilisation: its emergence from a socially isolated and culturally deaf semipatriarchal society, and its entrance into international and interlingual contacts and relationships. A multitude of different languages, cultures and times became available to Europe, and this became a decisive factor in its life and thought.[19]

There can be no doubting the influence that Bakhtin's discussion of the role of carnival in early modern letters has exercised on the study of popular culture. By rescuing the popular from the condescension of official canonical genres, it invested its role in everyday life with the philosophical seriousness it merits.[20] It is, however, the concepts he developed for the analysis of novelistic discourse that have resonated most tellingly with the concerns of contemporary cultural analysis. This is especially true of his concept of dialogism, the inter-orientation of different words and worlds, and, in the particular meaning he gave it, the novel's 'double-accented, double-styled *hybrid construction*' which he defined as follows:

> What we are calling a hybrid construction is an utterance that belongs, by its grammatical (syntactic) and compositional markers, to a single speaker, but that each actually contains mixed within it two utterances, two speech manners, two styles, two 'languages,' two semantic and axiological belief systems. We repeat, there is no formal – compositional and syntactic – boundary between these utterances, styles, languages, belief systems; the division of voices and languages takes

place within the limits of a single syntactic whole, often within the
limits of a simple sentence.[21]

It is no surprise, in the light of passages like this, that Bakhtin should
have been invoked as the patron saint of those who have attempted to
develop a new poetics based on the dialogic reciprocity of different
cultural perspectives and points of view. These endeavours have formed
a part and parcel of the post-1980s debates about globalization and the
greater fluidity of movements – of peoples and cultures – across
national boundaries. Nor is it surprising that his has been a name to
conjure with in accounts of the necessarily hybrid organization of
diasporic cultures, or of the diacritical structure of self and other that is
in play in any process of identity formation. Or that his work has been
invoked in discussions of the necessarily two-way processes that are
involved in relations of colonial exchange, or of the side-glancing quality of much contemporary visual culture as electronic media undermine the fixing of vision associated with traditional picture space. Not
surprising, perhaps, but remarkable all the same that such a lively and
productive orientation to the always mutually interpenetrating logic of
cultures-in-exchange and the always unpredictable new directions that
will result from such encounters should have come from an intellectual
whose own historical experience was of a regime whose imagination
was deeply monologic. Even more reason, then, to confirm his status as
a theoretical hero for our times.

NOTES

CHAPTER 1   CRITICISM AND LITERATURE

1   This aspect of Saussure's influence is discussed in T. Hawkes, *Structuralism and Semiotics* (London: Methuen, 1977) – a companion volume in this series.

2   F. R. Leavis, *The Common Pursuit* (Harmondsworth: Penguin, 1969), p. 213.

3   Lukács' most extended discussion of aesthetic questions is contained in his two-volumed *Ästhetik* (Berlin: Luchterhand, 1963). For a partial English translation, see 'Introduction to a Monograph on Aesthetics', *New Hungarian Quarterly*, Summer, 1964.

4   See P. Macherey and E. Balibar, 'On Literature as an Ideological Form: Some Marxist Propositions', *Oxford Literary Review*, vol. 3 no. I, 1978. A similar article, under Macherey's name only, appears as 'Problems of Reflection' in *Literature, Society and the Sociology of Literature* (University of Essex, 1977).

5   R. Williams, *Marxism and Literature* (Oxford: OUP, 1977), p. 145.

6   Ibid., p. 53.

CHAPTER 2   FORMALISM AND MARXISM

1   For details of the history, intellectual roots and organizational base of Russian Formalism, see V. Erlich, *Russian Formalism: History, Doctrine*

(The Hague: Mouton, 1955); E. M. Thompson, *Russian Formalism and Anglo-American New Criticism* (The Hague: Mouton, 1971) and K. Pomorska, *Russian Formalist Theory and its Poetic Ambience* (The Hague: Mouton, 1968).

2 The Formalists preferred to call themselves 'specifiers' as more accurately describing their overriding concern with the 'specificity' of literature. See V. Erlich, 'Russian Formalism', *Journal of the History of Ideas*, XXXIV (4), 1973, p. 67.

3 For a discussion of the relationship between Russian Formalism and New Criticism, see Thompson, op. cit. and the final chapter of Erlich *Russian Formalism: History, Doctrine*. Briefly, the differences between the two are:

(a) Whereas New Criticism subscribes to the neo-Kantian critique of positivism in arguing that the human sciences stand in need of qualitatively different methods from those employed in the natural sciences, the Formalists subscribed to a neo-positivist ideology in holding that the determination of the uniqueness of literature was a matter to be resolved solely by scientific and empirical methods.

(b) New Criticism, in arguing that the investigation of the uniqueness of literature can reveal something permanent and essential about the nature of Man, subscribes to a humanist ideology that was entirely alien to the Formalists.

(c) New Criticism has tended to stress the evocative and emotive – as opposed to the cognitive – function of poetic language and literary discourse.

4 See T. Hawkes, *Structuralism and Semiotics* (London: Routledge 2003), pp. 76–87 for a fuller discussion of Jakobson's work.

5 M. Twain, *The Adventures of Huckleberry Finn* (Harmondsworth: Penguin, 1972), pp. 145–6.

6 See Shklovsky, 'Art as Technique' in L. T. Lemon and M. J. Reis (eds), *Russian Formalist Criticism: Four Essays* (Lincoln: University of Nebraska Press, 1965).

7 See S. Heath, *The Nouveau Roman: A Study in the Practice of Writing* (London: Elek, 1972).

8 ibid., p. 33.

9 Shklovsky, op cit., p. 18.

10 This position was most forcefully and succinctly stated by Jakobson in his essay 'On Realism in Art', in L. Matejka and K. Pomorska (eds), *Readings in Russian Poetics* (Cambridge, Massachusetts: MIT Press, 1971).

11 See B. Brewster, 'From Shklovsky to Brecht', *Screen*, XV (2), 1974.

12 Cited in L. Matejka, 'On the First Russian Prologomena to Semiotics' in V. Vološinov, *Marxism and the Philosophy of Language* (New York: Seminar Press, 1973), p. 179.

13 R. Barthes, *Mythologies* (London: Cape, 1973), p. 112.

14 L. Trotsky, *Literature and Revolution* (Ann Arbor; Michigan: University of Michigan Press, 1960), p. 175.

15 For a useful introduction, see C. V. James, *Soviet Socialist Realism: Origins and Theory* (London: Macmillan, 1973).

16 It was partly to forestall such a reading of their work that Shklovsky, in developing his theory of prose, included a consideration of the defamiliarizing propensity embodied in certain of the devices constitutive of classical realism itself. See, for example, his 'The Mystery Novel: Dickens' "Little Dorrit" ', in Matejka and Pomorska (eds), op. cit.; 'The Connection between Devices of Sjuzet Construction and General Stylistic Devices', in S. Bann and S. Bowlt (eds) *Russian Formalism* (Edinburgh: Scottish Academic Press, 1973) and 'La Construction de la Nouvelle et du Roman' in Todorov (ed.), *Théorie de la Littérature: Textes des Formalistes Russes* (Paris: Editions de Seuil, 1965).

17 Shklovsky, op. cit., p. 12.

18 Cited in M. Enzenberger, 'Osip Brik: Selected Writings', *Screen*, XV (3), 1974, p. 51.

19 J. Mukařovský, 'Standard Language and Poetic Language' in D. C. Freeman (ed.), *Linguistics and Literary Style* (New York: Rinehart & Winston, 1970), p. 44.

20 For details, see 'Documents from *Lef*', *Screen*, XII (4), 1971; 'Documents from *Novy Lef*', *Screen*, XV (3), 1974; M. Pleynet, 'The "Left" Front of Arts: Eisenstein and the Old "Young Hegelians" ', *Screen*, XIII (I), 1972; and T. Todorov, 'Formalistes et Futuristes', *Tel Quel*, 1965.

21 Cited in Brewster, op. cit., p. 86.

22 Shklovsky was, for a time, militantly 'formalist', particularly during the period of his association with the Serapion Brotherhood. For details of this, see G. Kern and C. Collier (eds), *The Serapion Brotherhood: A Critical Anthology* (Ann Arbor; Michigan: University of Michigan Press, 1975).

23 See V. Erlich, *Russian Formalism: History, Doctrine* (The Hague: Mouton, 1955), pp. 110–17.

24 J. Tynyanov and R. Jakobson, 'Problems in the Study of Literature and Language', in Matejka and Pomorska (eds), op. cit., pp. 79–80.

25 See C. Lévi-Strauss, *The Elementary Structures of Kinship* (London: Eyre & Spottiswoode, 1970).

26 For a useful survey of semiotics and its difficulties in this area, see J. Kristeva, 'The System and the Speaking Subject', *Times Literary Supplement*, 12 October 1973.

27 This argument is also advanced in R. Seldon, 'Russian Formalism: An Unconcluded Dialogue', *Literature, Society and the Sociology of Literature* (University of Essex, 1977).

28 For details of the relevant conflicts within the BPRS, see H. Gallas, *Marxistische Literaturtheorie: Kontroversen im Bund des Proletarisches Revolutionärer Schriftstellers* (Berlin: Luchterhand, 1971). A partial translation of the chapter relating to Lukács exists as 'Georg Lukács and the League of Revolutionary Proletarian Writers', *Working Papers in Cultural Studies*, no. 4, 1973. For an introduction to some of the issues in the debate over Expressionism, see the exchange between Ernst Bloch and Georg Lukács in E. Bloch *et al.*, *Aesthetics and Politics* (London: New Left Books, 1978).

29 See the essays on Tolstoy in G. Lukács, *Studies in European Realism* (London: Hillway Publishing, 1950).

30 L. Althusser and E. Balibar, *Reading Capital* (London: New Left Books, 1970), p. 94.

CHAPTER 3   RUSSIAN FORMALISM

1 See R. Jakobson, 'On Russian Fairy Tales', *Selected Writings IV* (The Hague: Mouton, 1966), especially pp. 89–91; and R. Jakobson and P. Bogatyvev, 'On the Boundary between Studies of Folklore and Literature' in L. Matejka and K. Pomorska (eds), *Readings in Russian Poetics* (Cambridge, Massachusetts: MIT Press, 1971), p. 91.

2 F. de Saussure, *Course in General Linguistics* (London: Peter Owen, 1974), p. 3.

3 ibid., p. 8.

4 Cited in T. Todorov, 'Some Approaches to Russian Formalism', in S. Bann and S. Bowlt (eds), *Russian Formalism* (Edinburgh: Scottish Academic Press, 1973), pp. 7–8.

5 ibid., p.11.

6 V. Erlich, *Russian Formalism: History, Doctrine* (The Hague: Mouton, 1955), p. 176.

7 B. Eichenbaum, 'The Theory of the "Formal Method" ' in L. T. Lemon and M. J. Reis (eds), *Russian Formalist Criticism: Four Essays* (Lincoln: University of Nebraska Press, 1965), p. 117.

8 R. Seldon, 'Russian Formalism: an Unconcluded Dialogue' in *Litera-ture, Society and the Sociology of Literature* (University of Essex, 1977), p. 101.

9 'Documents from *Novy Lef*', *Screen*, XV (3), 1974, p. 67.

10 V. Shklovsky, *Mayakovsky and His Circle* (London: Pluto, 1974), p. 114.

11 J. Ortega y Gasset, *The Dehumanization of Art* (New Jersey: Princeton University Press, 1969), p. 21.

12 ibid., p. 38.

13 Shklovsky, op.cit., p. 68.

14 R. Jakobson, 'The Dominant' in Matejka and Pomorska (eds), op. cit., p. 87.

15 J. Tynyanov, 'On Literary Evolution', in Matejka and Pomorska (eds), op. cit., p. 69.

16 ibid, p. 67.

17 J. Culler, *Saussure* (London: Fontana, 1976), p. 36.

18 B. Eichenbaum, *The Young Tolstoy* (Ann Arbor, Michigan: Ardis, 1972), p. 18.

19 ibid., p. 100.

20 F. Jameson, *The Prison House of Language* (New Jersey: Princeton University Press, 1972), p. 18.

CHAPTER 4   FORMALISM AND BEYOND

1 R. Jakobson, 'On Realism in Art' in L. Matejka and K. Pomorska (eds), *Readings in Russian Poetics* (Cambridge, Massachusetts: MIT Press, 1971).

2 J. Tynyanov, 'On Literary Evolution' in ibid., p. 72.

3 K. Marx, *Grundrisse* (Harmondsworth: Penguin, 1973), pp. 110–11.

4 P. Macherey, 'Problems of Reflection' in *Literature, Society and the Sociology of Literature* (University of Essex, 1977), p. 45.

5 For a further elaboration of the concept of literary tradition as an active selection, see R. Williams, 'Base and Superstructure in Marxist Cultural Theory', *New Left Review*, 82, 1973.

6 R. Coward and J. Ellis, *Language and Materialism: Developments in Semiology and the Theory of the Subject* (London: Routledge & Kegan Paul, 1977), p.1.

7 T. Hawkes, *Structuralism and Semiotics* (London: Methuen, 1977), p. 16.

8 T. Todorov, 'Some Approaches to Russian Formalism' in S. Bann and S. Bowlt (eds), *Russian Formalism* (Edinburgh: Scottish Academic Press, 1973), p.9.

162 NOTES

9　F. de Saussure, *Course in General Linguistics* (London: Peter Owen, 1974), p. 77.

10　It has recently been suggested that Bakhtin was, in fact, the author of the works which appeared under Vološinov's name. As we are not in a position to ascertain whether or not this is true, we have followed the existing convention in referring to Vološinov and Bakhtin as separate persons.

11　V. Vološinov, *Marxism and the Philosophy of Language* (New York: Seminar Press, 1973), p. 53.

12　R. Williams, *Marxism and Literature* (Oxford: OUP, 1977), p. 37.

13　Vološinov, op. cit., p. 96.

14　ibid., p. 23.

15　ibid., p. 95.

16　From I. R. Titunik, 'The Formal Method and the Sociological Method' in ibid.

17　M. Bakhtin, *Problems of Dostoevsky's Poetics* (Ann Arbor, Michigan: Ardis, 1973), p. 88. (First published in 1929.)

18　ibid. See pp. 88–113.

19　M. Bakhtin, *Rabelais and His World* (Cambridge, Massachusetts: MIT Press, 1968), p.6.

20　ibid., p. 72.

21　Rabelais, *Gargantua and Pantagruel* (Harmondsworth: Penguin, 1970), Book One, chapter 17, p. 75.

22　ibid., Book One, chapter 4, pp. 47–8.

23　ibid., Book One, chapter 6, p. 52.

24　Bakhtin, *Rabelais and His World*, p. 226.

25　ibid., p. 465.

26　For a discussion of these developments and some extrapolations concerning their literary consequences, see H. Febvre and H. J. Martin, *The Coming of the Book: The Impact of Printing, 1450–1800* (London: New Left Books, 1976).

CHAPTER 5　MARXISM VERSUS AESTHETICS

1　See J. Kristeva, 'The Ruin of a Poetics' in S. Bann and S. Bowlt (eds), *Russian Formalism* (Edinburgh: Scottish Academic Press, 1973) for a notable exception.

2　This concept of the 'break' – or 'epistemological rupture' – in Marx's work was first introduced in Althusser's *For Marx* (Harmondsworth: Allen Lane, 1969).

3 See P. Anderson, *Considerations on Western Marxism* (London: New Left Books, 1976).

4 For a complete anthology, see K. Marx and F. Engels, *On Literature and Art* (Moscow: Progress Publishers, 1976).

5 Anderson, op. cit., p. 6.

6 ibid., p. 78.

7 ibid., p. 53.

8 C. MacCabe, 'Theory and Film: Principles of Realism and Pleasure', *Screen*, XVII (3), 1976, p. 10.

9 T. Eagleton, *Criticism and Ideology* (London: New Left Books, 1976,) p. 43.

CHAPTER 6   SCIENCE, LITERATURE AND IDEOLOGY

1 L. Althusser, *For Marx* (Harmondsworth: Allen Lane, 1969), p. 166.

2 ibid., p. 167.

3 Contained, respectively, in Althusser's *For Marx* and *Lenin and Philosophy* (London: New Left Books, 1971).

4 Althusser, *Lenin and Philosophy*, p. 158.

5 From the 1859 Preface to *A Contribution to the Critique of Political Economy*, cited in T. B. Bottomore and M. Rubel (eds), *Karl Marx: Selected Writings in Sociology and Social Philosophy* (Harmondsworth: Penguin, 1965), p. 67.

6 N. Poulantzas, *Classes in Contemporary Capitalism* (London: New Left Books, 1975), p. 28.

7 Althusser, *Lenin and Philosophy*, p. 138.

8 Althusser, *For Marx*, p. 235.

9 L. Althusser, *Essays in Self-Criticism* (London: New Left Books, 1976), p. 56.

10 See, in particular, Althusser's essay on 'Marx's Relation to Hegel' in *Politics and History* (London: New Left Books, 1972).

11 This argument is outlined most fully in L. Althusser, 'The Conditions of Marx's Scientific Discovery', *Theoretical Practice*, 7/8, 1963.

12 The first of these is in *For Marx*; the others in *Lenin and Philosophy*.

13 Althusser, *Lenin and Philosophy*, p. 206.

14 ibid., p. 204.

15 ibid., p. 204.

16 ibid., p. 203.

17 ibid., p. 219.

18 ibid., p. 205.

19 ibid., p. 205.

20 There is, in this respect, a close relationship between Althusser's position and that of such theorists as Julia Kristeva who, working in the orbit of Jacques Lacan's re-reading of Freud, have sought to reveal the mechanisms by which, at the level of the psyche, literary works disrupt or unhinge the mental grip of ideological categories. Unfortunately, an examination of these relationships would take us beyond the boundaries of this study. For an introduction, however, see R. Coward and J. Ellis, *Language and Materialism* (London: Routledge & Kegan Paul, 1977).

CHAPTER 7 THE LEGACY OF AESTHETICS

1 L. Althusser, *Lenin and Philosophy* (London: New Left Books, 1971), p. 206.

2 'An Interview with Pierre Macherey', *Red Letters,* no. 5, Summer 1977, p. 3.

3 F. Mulhern, 'Marxism in Literary Criticism', *New Left Review*, 108, 1978, p. 82.

4 For a further development of this perspective, see B. Hindess and P. Q. Hirst, *Mode of Production and Social Formation* (London: Macmillan, 1977).

5 See J. Rancière, 'On the Theory of Ideology', *Radical Philosophy*, VII, Spring, 1974. See also P. Q. Hirst, 'Althusser and the Theory of Ideology', *Economy and Society*, V (4), 1976, p. 397.

6 See Althusser's *Essays in Self-Criticism* (London: New Left Books, 1976).

CHAPTER 8 WORK IN PROGRESS

1 V. Shklovsky, 'Art as Technique' in L. T. Lemon and M. J. Reis (eds), *Russian Formalist Criticism: Four Essays* (Lincoln: University of Nebraska Press, 1965), p. 18.

2 T. Eagleton, *Criticism and Ideology* (London: New Left Books, 1976), p. 42.

3 F. Mulhern, 'Marxism in Literary Criticism', *New Left Review*, 108, 1978, p. 78.

4 Eagleton, op. cit., p. 101.

5 ibid., p. 48.

6 ibid., p. 53.

7   ibid., pp 166–7.

8   ibid., p. 180.

9   ibid., p. 181.

10 ibid., p. 180.

11 ibid., p. 125.

12 ibid., p. 126.

13 ibid., p. 181.

14 ibid., p. 77.

15 ibid., p. 177.

16 ibid., p. 98.

17 ibid., pp 83–94 for Eagleton's discussion of Macherey.

18 P. Macherey, 'Problems of Reflection' in *Literature, Society and Sociology of Literature* (University of Essex, 1977), p. 52.

19 'An Interview with Pierre Macherey' in *Red Letters*, 5, Summer, 1977, p. 3.

20 P. Macherey and E. Balibar, 'Sur Littérature Comme Forme Idéologique: Quelque Hypothèses Marxistes', *Littérature*, 14, 1974.

21 ibid.

22 R. Balibar, 'An Example of Literary Work in France: George Sand's "La Mare Au Diable"/"The Devil's Pool" of 1846', in F. Barker *et al.* (eds), *The Sociology of Literature: 1848* (University of Essex Press, 1978), p. 28.

23 See, for example, T. Davies, 'Education, Ideology and Literature', *Red Letters*, 7, 1978.

24 R. Balibar, op. cit., p. 42.

25 'An Interview with Pierre Macherey', op. cit., p. 7.

26 R. Balibar, op. cit., pp. 29–30.

27 ibid., p. 35.

28 XIth Thesis on Feuerbach, *The German Ideology* (London: Lawrence & Wishart, 1965), p. 667.

AFTERWORD

1   I draw here on some retrospective formulations written shortly after the book was first published: see Bennett, T., '*Formalism and Marxism* Revisited', *Southern Review*, 15 (1), 1982.

2   Hartley, J, and Hawkes, T., 'Popular Culture and High Culture', *Mass Communications and Society* (Milton Keynes: The Open University Press, 1977). It was characteristic of Terry Hawkes's openness and generosity of spirit that his invitation to me to contribute a title to the *New Accents* series arose out of these exchanges.

3 See Bennett, T., *Outside Literature* (London and New York: Routledge, 1990).

4 See, for one of the most illuminating discussion of these processes, Guillory, J., *Cultural Capital: The Problem of Literary Canon Formation* (Chicago and London: University of Chicago Press, 1993).

5 And one I contributed to in later work: see Bennett, T., 'Texts in History: The Determination of Readings and their Texts', in R. Young and D. Attridge (eds) *(1987) Post-Structuralism and History* (Cambridge: Cambridge University Press, 1987), and Bennett, T. and Woollacott, J., *Bond and Beyond: The Political Career of a Popular Hero* London: Macmillan, 1987.

6 Eagleton, T., *Criticism and Ideology: A Study in Marxist Literary Theory* (London: New Left Books, 1976), p. 44.

7 Eagleton, T., *The Ideology of the Aesthetic* (Oxford: Blackwell, 1990), p. 9.

8 Poovey, M., *A History of the Modern Fact: Problems of Knowledge in the Sciences of Wealth and Society* (Chicago and London: University of Chicago Press, 1998).

9 Bourdieu, P., *The Rules of Art: Genesis and Structure of the Literary Field* (Cambridge: Polity Press, 1996), p. 200.

10 ibid., p. 201.

11 ibid., p. 201.

12 ibid., p. 288.

13 Williams, R., *Keywords: A Vocabulary of Culture and Society* (London: Fontana/Croom Helm, 1976), p. 22.

14 Williams, R., *Marxism and Literature* (Oxford: Oxford University Press, 1977), pp. 35–42.

15 See chapter 5, note 1.

16 The most easily accessible of these are included in the third section of the revised bibliography I have prepared for this edition.

17 See, for a brief discussion, Holquist, M., *Dialogism: Bakhtin and His World* (London and New York: Routledge, 1990), pp. 192–5. In Holquist's view, 90% of the disputed texts published under the names of Medvedev and Vološinov are likely to have been written by Bakhtin.

18 Bakhtin, M. M., *The Dialogic Imagination: Four Essays* (Austin: University of Texas Press, 1981), p. 10.

19 ibid., p. 11.

20 Stalleybrass, P. and White, A., *The Politics and Poetics of Transgression* (London: Methuen, 1986) has been perhaps the most influential text of this kind. Its discussion of Bakhtin's analysis of carnival as a

counterpoint to Jürgen Habermas's account of the public sphere has been a significant springboard for the analysis of a number of contemporary television genres, especially talk shows.

21   Bakhtin, *The Dialogic Imagination*, pp. 304–5.

BIBLIOGRAPHY

My concern in this Bibliography is to guide the reader who is interested in following up the debates introduced in this study. It falls into three sections. In the first, I list those works of the Russian Formalists which are most easily available in English translation together with details of the most easily accessible commentaries on the Russian Formalists. Readers interested in the more general contribution which Russian Formalism has made to the development of structuralism and semiotics could usefully consult the bibliography in Terence Hawkes, *Structuralism and Semiotics* (London: Routledge, 2003). In Section 2, I list the works of Louis Althusser, Pierre Macherey and Terry Eagleton which most clearly represent the concerns of Althusserian literary theory. Some critical commentaries on this tradition are also included as well as sources reflecting its influence. Section 3 identifies relevant works by Mikhail Bakhtin, Valentin Vološinov and other members of the Bakhtin school. I have updated all three sections to take account of the main studies – or at least those that I know of – that have appeared over the period since *Formalism and Marxism* was first published. In the case of Bakhtin, however, I have limited my attention to works that engage with Bakhtin from the perspective of the issues engaged with in this study. The influence of Bakhtin's work has, however, been a much broader one, with significant impacts on post-colonial studies, carnival and popular culture and the dialogic organization of social life more generally.

SECTION ONE: RUSSIAN FORMALISM

Any, C.J. *Boris Eikhenbaum : Voices of a Russian Formalist* (Stanford, Calif: Stanford University Press, 1994).

Bann, S. and Bowlt, S. (eds.), *Russian Formalism* (Edinburgh: Scottish Academic Press, 1973)

Brewster, B., 'From Shklovsky to Brecht: A Reply', *Screen*, XV (2), Summer, 1974.

Brewster, B. (ed.), 'Documents from *Lef*' *Screen*, XII (4), 1974.

Brewster, B. (ed.), 'Documents from *Novy Lef*', *Screen*, XV (3), 1974.

Culler, J., *Structuralist Poetics: Structuralism, Linguistics and the Study of Literature* (London: Routledge & Kegan Paul, 1975).

Eichenbaum, B., *The Young Tolstoy* (Ann Arbor, Michigan: Ardis, 1972).

Erlich, V., *Russian Formalism: History, Doctrine* (The Hague: Mouton, 1955).

Erlich, V., 'Russian Formalism', *Journal of the History of Ideas*, XXXIV (4), 1973.

Enzenberger, M., 'Osip Brik, Selected Writings of the *Novy Lef* Period', *Screen*, XV (3), 1974.

Garson, J., 'Literary History: Russian Formalist Views, 1916–1928', *Journal of the History of Ideas*, XXXI (3), 1970.

Gourfinkel, N., 'Les Nouvelles Méthodes d'Histoire Littéraire en Russie', *Le Monde Slave*, VI, 1929.

Jakobson, R., *Selected Writings* (4 vols) (The Hague, Mouton, 1962–).

Jackson, R.L. and Rudy, S. (eds) *Russian Formalism : A Retrospective Glance: A Festschrift in Honor of Victor Erlich* (New Haven and Columbus, Ohio: Yale Center for International and Area Studies, 1985).

Jameson, F., *The Prison-House of Language: A Critical Account of Structuralism and Russian Formalism* (New Jersey: Princeton University Press, 1972).

Kern, G. and Collier, C. (eds.), *The Serapion Brotherhood: A Critical Anthology* (Ann Arbor, Michigan: University of Michigan Press, 1975).

Lemon, L. T. and Reis, M. J. (eds.), *Russian Formalist Criticism: Four Essays* (Lincoln, University of Nebraska Press, 1965).

Matejka, L. and Pomorska, K. (eds.), *Readings in Russian Poetics* (Cambridge, Massachusetts: MIT Press, 1971).

O'Toole, L.M. and Shukman A. (eds) *Formalism : History, Comparison, Genre* (Oxford : Holdan Books, 1978).

Pleynet, M., 'The "Left" Front of Art: Einstein and the old "Young Hegelians" ', *Screen*, XIII (1), 1972.

Pomorska, K., *Russian Formalist Theory and its Poetic Ambiance* (The Hague: Mouton, 1968).

Seldon, R., 'Russian Formalism: An Unconcluded Dialogue', in *Literature, Society and the Sociology of Literature* (University of Essex Press, 1977).

Shklovsky, V., *A Sentimental Journey: Memoirs, 1917–1922* (Ithaca and London: Cornell University Press, 1970).

Shklovsky, V., *Zoo: Or Letters Not About Love* (Ithaca and London: Cornell University Press, 1971).

Shklovsky, V., *Mayakovsky and His Circle* (London: Pluto, 1974).

Steiner, P., *Russian Formalism: A Metapoetics* (Ithaca: Cornell University Press, 1984).

Striedter, J., *Literary Structure, Evolution, and Value: Russian Formalism and Czech Structuralism Reconsidered* (Cambridge, Massachusetts, and London: Harvard University Press, 1989).

Thompson, E. M., *Russian Formalism and Anglo-American New Criticism* (The Hague: Mouton, 1971).

Todorov, T. (ed.), *Théorie de la Littérature: Textes des Formalistes Russes* (Paris: Editions de Seuil, 1965).

Todorov, T., 'Formalistes et Futuristes', *Tel Quel*, XXXV, 1965.

Tomashevskij, B., 'La Nouvelle École d'Histoire Littéraire en Russie', *Revue des Études Slaves*, VII, 1928.

Trotsky, L., 'The Formalist School of Poetry', *Literature and Revolution* (Ann Arbor, Michigan: University of Michigan Press, 1960).

Tynyanov, J., 'The Notion of Construction', *New Left Review*, 43, 1967.

Voznesenskij, A. N., 'Problems of Method in the Study of Literature in Russia', *Slavonic Review*, VI, 1927.

SECTION TWO: ALTHUSSERIAN MARXISM AND LITERARY CRITICISM

Althusser, L., 'The Conditions of Marx's Scientific Discovery', *Theoretical Practice*, 7/8, 1963.

Althusser, L., *For Marx* (Harmondsworth: Allen Lane, 1969).

Althusser, L., *Lenin and Philosophy, and Other Essays* (London: New Left Books, 1971).

Althusser, L., *Politics and History* (London: New Left Books, 1972).

Althusser, L., *Essays in Self-Criticism* (London: New Left Books, 1976).

Althusser, L. and Balibar, E., *Reading Capital* (London: New Left Books, 1970).

Baker, F., Hulme, P., Iveson, M. and Loxley, D. (eds) *Literature, Politics and Theory: Papers from the Essex Conference 1976–84* (London: Methuen, 1986).

Balibar, R., *Les Français Fictifs: Le Rapport des Styles Littéraires au Français National* (Paris: Librarie Hachette, 1974).

Balibar, R., 'An Example of Literary Work in France: George Sand's "La Mare Au Diable"/"The Devil's Pool" of 1946' in F. Barker, *et al.* (eds.), *The Sociology of Literature: 1848* (University of Essex Press, 1978).

Balibar, R. and Laporte, D., *Le Français National: Politique et Practique de la Langue Nationale sur la Révolution* (Paris: Librarie Hachette, 1974).

Bennett, T. 'Marxism and Popular Fiction', *Literature and History*, 7 (2), 1981.

Bennett, T. 'Texts, Readers, Reading Formations', *Literature and History*, 9 (2), 1983

Callinicos, A., *Althusser's Marxism* (London: Pluto, 1976).

Doyle, B. *English and Englishness* (London: Routledge, 1989).

Eagleton, T., *Myths of Power: A Marxist Study of the Brontës* (London: Macmillan, 1975).

Eagleton, T., *Marxism and Literary Criticism* (London: Methuen, 1976).

Eagleton, T., *Criticism and Ideology* (London: New Left Books, 1976).

Eagleton, T., 'Ecriture and Eighteenth-Century Fiction', in *Literature, Society and the Sociology of Literature* (University of Essex Press, 1977).

Eagleton, T., 'Tennyson: Politics and Sexuality in *The Princess* and *In Memoriam*' in F. Barker, *et al.* (eds.), *The Sociology of Literature: 1848* (University of Essex Press, 1978).

Eagleton, T., 'Marxist Literary Criticism' in H. Scheff (ed.), *Contemporary Approaches to English Studies* (London: Heinemann, 1977).

Frow, J. *Marxism and Literary History* (Cambridge, Massachusetts: Harvard University Press, 1986).

Goldstein, P., *The Politics of Literary Criticism: An Introduction to Marxist Cultural Theory* (Tallahassee: University of Florida Press, 1990).

Hall, S., 'Culture, the Media and the "Ideology Effect"', in J. Curran, M. Gurevitch and J. Woollacott (eds.), *Massachusetts Communication and Society* (London: Arnold, 1977).

Hirst, P. Q., 'Althusser and the Theory of Ideology', *Economy and Society*, V (4), 1976.

Hitchcock, P. *Working-Class Fiction in Theory and Practice* (Ann Arbor and London: UMI Research Press).

Humm, P., Stigant, P. and Widdowson, P. (eds) *Popular Fictions: Essays in Literature and History* (London: Methuen, 1986).

Macherey, P., *A Theory of Literary Production* (London: Routledge & Kegan Paul, 1978) (First published in France, 1966).

Macherey, P., 'Problems of Reflection' in *Literature, Society and the Sociology of Literature* (University of Essex Press, 1977).

Macherey, P. – an interview given in *Red Letters*, no.5., Summer, 1977.

Macherey, P. and Balibar, E., 'On Literature as an Ideological Form: Some Marxist Propositions', *Oxford Literary Review*, vol.3, no.1, 1978.

Mulhern, F., 'Marxism in Literary Criticism', *New Left Review*, 108, 1978.

Pêcheux, M. *Language, Semantics and Ideology* (London: Macmillan, 1982).

Rancière, J., 'On the Theory of Ideology', *Radical Philosophy*, VII, Spring, 1974.

Resch, R.P., *Althusser and the Renewal of Marxist Social Theory* (Berkeley, Los Angeles and London: University of California Press, 1992).

Widdowson, P. (ed) *Re-Reading English* (London: Methuen, 1982).

Widdowson, P. *Hardy in History: A Study in Literary Sociology* (London: Routledge, 1989).

SECTION THREE: THE BAKHTIN SCHOOL

Bakhtin, M. M., *Rabelais and His World* (Cambridge, Massachusetts: MIT Press, 1968).

Bakhtin, M. M., *Problems of Dostoevsky's Poetics* (Ann Arbor, Michigan: Ardis, 1973).

Bakhtin, M. M., *The Word in the Novel* (Cambridge : Cambridge University Press, 1980).

Bakhtin, M. M., *Speech Genres and Other Late Essays* (Austin : University of Texas Press, 1986).

Bakhtin, M. M., *The Dialogic Imagination: Four Essays by M. M. Bakhtin* (Austin: University of Texas Press, 1981).

Bakhtin, M. M., *Art and Answerability : Early Philosophical Essays* (Austin : University of Texas Press, 1990).

Bender, J. *Imagining the Penitentiary: Fiction and the Architecture of Mind in Eighteenth-Century England* (Chicago and London: University of Chicago Press, 1987).

Clarke, K. and Holquist, M. *Mikhail Bakhtin* (Cambridge, Massachusetts: The Belknap Press of Harvard University Press, 1984).

Holquist, M. *Dialogism: Bakhtin and his World* (London and New York: Routledge, 1990).

Medvedev, P.N./Bakhtin, M. M. *The Formal Method in Literary Scholarship: A Critical Introduction to Sociological Poetics* (Baltimore and London: Johns Hopkins University Press, 1978).

Morris, P. (ed) *The Bakhtin Reader : Selected Writings of Bakhtin, Medvedev and Voloshinov* (London : E. Arnold, 1994).

Pechey, G. 'Bakhtin, Marxism and Post-Structuralism' in Barker, F. *et al* (eds) *Literature, Politics and Theory: Papers from the Essex Conference 1976–84* (London: Methuen, 1986).

Pechey, G. 'On the Borders of Bakhtin: Dialogization, Decolonisation', *Oxford Literary Review* 9(1–2), 1987.

Shukman, A. *Between Marxism and Formalism : The Stylistics of Mikhail Bakhtin* (Cambridge: Cambridge University Press, 1980).

Shukman, A. (ed) *Bakhtin School Papers*, special issue of *Russian Poetics in Translation*, no. 10, 1983.

Todorov, T. *Mikhail Bakhtin: The Dialogical Principle* (Manchester: Manchester University Press, 1984).

Vološinov, V., *Marxism and the Philosophy of Language* (New York: Seminar Press, 1973).

Vološinov, V., *Freudianism: A Marxist Critique* (New York: Academic Press, 1976).

INDEX

Adorno, Theodor 83
The Adventures of Huckleberry Finn
(Twain) 17–19
Aeschylus 56
aesthetics 13, 35, 89, 115, 139,
149–53; aesthetic mode 10;
Althusser 98; bourgeois 80, 81,
84, 86, 116, 117, 120; concept of
6, 7, 12; cultural studies 143;
Formalism 54, 56; Marxism 3, 77,
83, 84–5, 88, 147–8
Althusser, Louis 79, 81, 86, 127, 138,
146–7; aesthetic mode 10;
critique of 103–4, 107–9, 111,
116–18; declining influence 143;
Eagleton comparison 121, 124;
'expressive totality' 32–3;
ideology 34, 90–4, 96, 99, 103–6,
109, 111–14, 117–18; influence
121; literature 7, 89, 97–102,
104–6, 108–9, 111–13, 117–18,
139–40; 'overdetermination' 33;

'practices' 90–1, 106–7; science
96–7, 99, 102, 103–4; social
formation 30
Althusserians 10, 13–14, 79, 85, 88,
104
Anderson, Perry 82, 83
Arnold, Matthew 130
art: aesthetic knowledge 10;
Althusser 97–9, 108; 'art-for-art's
sake' 16, 21, 25, 26–7;
'dehumanization' 45; Greek
55–6; history of 53; Russian
Formalism 23, 27
avant-garde 19–20, 79, 110

Bakhtin, Mikhail 23, 152–5;
'carnivalization of literature'
67–8; on Dostoevsky 62–3;
historical poetics 61, 66, 144, 153;
identity 162n; literature as a
historically specific practice of
writing 67, 73–4, 118; 'practical

criticism' 79; on Rabelais 67, 68–74, 77; 'renewal' concept 73, 74, 78; *see also* Vološinov

Bakhtin school 14, 144, 152

Balibar, Étienne 11, 55, 127–8

Balibar, Renée 128–33

Balzac, Honoré de 56

Barthes, Roland 19, 23, 78

Baumgarten, Alexander 150

belles lettres 16, 37, 67, 73, 78, 108, 118, 125

Benjamin, Walter 83

Bertolazzi, Carlo 98

bestrangement 51, 52

Bolsheviks 24

Bourdieu, Pierre 149, 151–2

bourgeois humanism 94, 95, 100, 133

Brecht, Bertolt 22, 78, 84, 98, 100, 114

Brik, Osip 26

Bund des Proletarisches Revolutionärer Schriftstellers 30

capitalism 92–3, 123, 129, 150, 152

carnival 67, 68, 70, 72, 153, 154

Cervantes, Miguel de 74

class struggle 66, 97, 112, 129

colonialism 101–2

communism 95, 111

Conrad, Joseph 124

Cremonini, Leonardo 98

criticism and politics 110, 111–15, 118–19, 120, 135–6

Culler, Jonathan 49

cultural practice 10, 12, 35, 55, 135

cultural studies 143

culture 11–12, 58, 141, 151

defamiliarization 7, 17–18, 22, 40–1,
43–4, 45–6, 73; *avant-garde* 20, 78–9; carnival 67; Futurism 25, 26; literary function 54, 105, 106, 145, 146; 'renewal' concept 78

Deighton, Len 17

Della Volpe, Galvano 83

The Devil's Pool (Sand) 131–3, 134

diachronic/synchronic 42, 52, 58–9

Dickens, Charles 114, 121, 124

'the dominant' 43, 46, 54

Dostoevsky, Fyodor 47–8, 62–3

Dürer, Albrecht 133

Eagleton, Terry 7, 79, 103, 117, 127, 138; aesthetics 10, 149–50; function of criticism 119; ideology 104, 105, 114, 123–6, 140, 146, 147; literary criticism 86–8; literary modes of production 121–6, 141; literary value 124, 125, 140

Eichenbaum, Boris 15, 21–2, 41, 42, 50–2, 145

Eliot, George 114, 124

Eliot, T. S. 124

empiricism 8, 38, 40, 87

Engels, Friedrich 82, 92

Erlich, Victor 22, 28, 42

Eurocommunism 111

Expressionism 30

Fielding, Henry 11

folk humour 67–9, 72, 73, 74

foregrounding, mechanisms of 26, 99, 100, 105

Formalism, Russian 3, 13–14, 45–6, 116, 144, 146–7; accomplishments of 53–7; Althusser comparison 99–100, 103–6; 'art-for-art's sake' 25–6;

basic principles 16–21; Bourdieu 151–2; cognition 44; Futurism 25–7, 43; history of 15–16, 21–2; linguistics 36, 37, 38; literature as science 39–40; Marxist criticism relationship 22–3, 30–1, 32, 34, 77–80, 117, 147; New Criticism 16, 158n; problem of literary evolution 28, 49–52, 56–7; structuralism 22, 29–30, 37; uniqueness of literature 7
Freud, Sigmund 164n
Futurists 24–7, 30, 43

Gargantua and Pantagruel (Rabelais) 68–74
Goethe, Johann Wolfgang von 51
Goldmann, Lucien 83, 152
Gorky, Maxim 24
Goya, Francisco 133
Gramsci, Antonio 83
'grotesque realism' 69

Hartley, John 144, 145
Hawkes, Terence 57, 144, 145
Heath, Stephen 19, 20
Hegel, Georg Wilhelm Friedrich 31, 80, 84, 97
Hobbes, Thomas 80
Holbein, Hans 132, 133
Homer 12, 55, 56
hybrid construction 154–5

idealism 58, 96, 147; aesthetics 7; Althusser 106–7, 109, 116–17, 118; Eagleton 121; Marxism 81, 85
ideological state apparatuses 92, 93
ideology 7, 10, 11, 114–15, 131; aesthetic 122; Althusser 34, 90–4, 96, 99, 103–6, 109, 111–14,

117–18; Eagleton 104, 105, 123–6, 140, 146, 147; Macherey 101, 102; Marxism 81, 88; medieval 67–8, 69, 70, 73, 74, 114; social totality 33; Vološinov 64
inter-textuality 49, 146, 149
interpretative criticism 86–7

Jakobson, Roman 15, 27, 40, 45–6, 53; Czech structuralism 22, 29, 37; literary evolution 28–9; poetry 16–17, 37, 57; realism 43
James, Henry 124
Jameson, Fredric 52, 150
Joyce, James 19, 121

Kafka, Franz 12, 19
Kant, Immanuel 16, 21, 26
Kautsky, Karl 82
knowledge 10, 99, 112, 113; art 98, 108; empiricism 87; ideology 88; scientific 96–7
Kristeva, Julia 153, 164n

Labriola, Antonio 82
Lacan, Jacques 164n
la langue 37, 39, 42, 46, 57–8, 105; change 50, 60; critique of 59–61, 62, 64–6; *see also* diachronic/ synchronic
Laporte, Dominique 128–31
Leavis, Frank Raymond 9, 55, 86, 130
Lef 25, 27
Lenin, Vladimir Ilyich 81, 82
Lévi-Strauss, Claude 29
linguistics 4, 16, 39, 42, 57; critique of Saussurian 57–62, 63–6; and literature 36–8; *see also la langue*
literariness 16, 28, 34, 66, 105, 147;

abstract character of 46; inter-
textuality 48–9; literary systems
54; object of inquiry 40; as
ultimate concern of Formalists
38; *see also* defamiliarization;
literary system
literary criticism: defamiliarization
40–1; discourses of 4, 5–8, 9, 13,
137–8; *see also* Marxist criticism
literary function 41, 42–3, 54–5, 78,
108; defamiliarization 54, 105,
106, 145, 146; shifts in 48; text's
place in literary system 46, 47,
60, 74, 105
literary system 46–7, 54, 55, 60–1,
78, 105; Bakhtin 74; Bourdieu 151,
152; defamiliarization 146
literary tradition 55
literary/non-literary 6, 7, 8, 10–11,
12, 40–1, 85
literature: Althusser 89, 97–102,
104–6, 108–9, 111–13, 117–18,
139–40; concepts of 3, 4, 5–8,
9–14, 35, 138–41; Formalism/
Marxism comparison 79–80;
France 128–30; as historical
category 67–74; ideology 114–15;
Macherey 127–8; Marxism 84, 85,
86, 88–9, 147–8; modes of
literary production 121–6, 141;
popular fiction distinction 144–5;
'reality' 44; reflection theory 31–2;
Russian Formalism 16–17, 20–2,
27, 34, 39–41, 45–6, 53–4, 146;
social practice relationship 33–4
Lukács, Georg 10, 24, 83, 84, 110,
150; Aristotelian concept of
mimesis 32; social totality 33; on
Tolstoy 31; world-view analysis 31,
152

MacCabe, Colin 87
Macherey, Pierre 10, 11, 79, 103, 117,
127–8; 'fiction effect' 139, 140–1;
Greek art 55; idealism 58; on Jules
Verne 100–2; literary criticism
86–8; literature 7, 108, 146;
science 87
Marcuse, Herbert 83, 84
Marlowe, Christopher 11
Marx, Karl Heinrich 31, 81–2, 84,
109, 134, 142; eternal value of
Greek art 55–6; history 97;
ideology 92; the state 80–1;
'theoretical break' 81, 82
Marxist criticism 3, 14, 16, 30–5,
77–89, 116, 138; aesthetics 83,
84–5, 147–8, 149–50; decline 143;
dependency on bourgeois
criticism and aesthetics 11, 81;
early Soviet forms of 21;
historical poetics 61; literary
modes of production 141;
literature concepts 7, 8, 10, 13;
metaphysic of the text 56, 120;
politics 84, 111, 114–15, 135–6;
Russian Formalism relationship
22–3, 30–1, 32, 34, 77–80, 117,
147; *see also* Althusser; Bakhtin
mass culture 11, 108
materialism 67, 82, 83, 88, 107, 120;
aesthetics 80, 85, 86, 147, 148;
Althusser 90–1, 96, 106;
Eagleton 121, 125; ideology 10, 81;
'of production/consumption' 77
Mayakovsky, Vladimir 25
Medvedev, Pavel 23, 61, 66, 153
Mehring, Franz 82
metaphor 42
Michelangelo 133
mimesis 17, 32

misrecognition 10, 88, 95, 102, 109, 113

Moscow Linguistic Circle 15, 16, 25

Mother Courage (Brecht) 100

Mukařovský, Jan 26, 27

Mulhern, Francis 110

neo-Kantianism 158n

New Criticism 16, 158n

nouveau-roman 19–20

novels 54–5, 153–4

Novy Lef 25, 27, 43

OPOYAZ *see* Society for the Investigation of Poetic Language

Ortega y Gasset, José 44–5, 95

ostranenie 43; *see also* defamiliarization

la parole 39, 59

Parsons, Talcott 151

Plekhanov, Georgy 82

poetry 16–17, 21, 37, 42, 45, 57

politics 22, 134; criticism and 110, 111–15, 118–19, 120, 135–6; Marxism 84, 111, 114–15, 135–6; texts' political effects 77, 119

Poovey, Mary 150–1

popular culture 11, 73, 108

Poulantzas, Nicos 92–3

problematic 40, 80

Proletkult 24

Rabelais, François 67, 68–74, 77

Rancière, Jacques 112

realism 19–20, 21, 24, 43, 54; 'grotesque' 69; political value 110

reflection theory 21, 32, 54, 103

Renaissance 67, 68, 69, 73, 74, 114, 153

Richardson, Samuel 11

Robbe-Grillet, Alain 20, 43

romanticism 51, 52

Rousseau, Jean-Jacques 51

Russian Association of Proletarian Writers 24

Sand, George 131–3, 134

Sartre, Jean Paul 83

Saussure, Ferdinand de: critique of 50, 57–62, 63, 64–6; diachronic/synchronic 42, 58–9; influence 4; *langue/parole* 36–7, 39, 42, 46, 50, 57–61, 63, 64; signifier/signified 4–5, 42, 49, 63; theory of science 38–9

Schiller, Friedrich von 84

science 38–9, 115; Althusser 96–7, 99, 102, 103–4; ideology relationship 109, 111–13, 114; Macherey 87

Scott, Sir Walter 51

Seldon, Ray 43, 61

semiotics 22, 64, 78

Sevastopol Sketches (Tolstoy) 51–2

Shakespeare, William 11, 56, 110–11

Shklovsky, Viktor 15, 20, 21–2, 23, 27, 99, 117; art-for-art's sake 25–6; canonization of the junior branch 47, 144–5; *fabula/sjuzet* 100; literary works 45, 50; recognition 44; Serapion Brotherhood 159n; on Sterne's *Tristram Shandy* 19; theory of prose 159n; *zaum* poetry 21

signification 4–5, 8, 16–17, 21, 54, 64, 92

signifier/signified 4–5, 34, 42, 45, 49, 63, 105

skaz 62

social formation 30, 90, 91, 123
socialist realism 22
Society for the Investigation of Poetic Language (OPOYAZ) 15, 16, 25, 37
Spinoza, Benedictus de 112
Stendhal, Marie Henri Beyle 51
Sterne, Laurence 19, 51
structuralism 22, 29–30, 36–7, 78, 86; Marxist criticism 23; Saussure 57, 58
synchronic/diachronic 42, 52, 58–9

Tel Quel 78
text, metaphysic of 49, 56, 119–20, 128, 131, 134–5, 148
Todorov, Tzvetan 22, 58
Tolstoy, Leo 31, 50–2
Tristram Shandy (Sterne) 19

Trotsky, Leon 23–4, 82
Twain, Mark 17–18
Tynyanov, Jurij 15, 27, 28–9, 46–7, 54, 55

Verne, Jules 100–2
Vološinov, Valentin 23, 153; critique of Saussure 61–6; identity 162n; ideology 64; la langue 64–6; see also Bakhtin
The Voyeur (Robbe-Grillet) 43

War and Peace (Tolstoy) 51
Williams, Raymond 11–13, 14, 63, 153
world-view analysis 31, 152

zaum poetry 21
Zhdanov, Andrei 22